Collins

KEY CONCEPTS IN

Psychology

Kay Kendall

William Collins' dream of knowledge for all began with the publication of his first book in 1819. A self-educated mill worker, he not only enriched millions of lives, but also founded a flourishing publishing house. Today, staying true to this spirit, Collins books are packed with inspiration, innovation and practical expertise. They place you at the centre of a world of possibility and give you exactly what you need to explore it.

Collins. Freedom to teach

Published by Collins
An imprint of HarperCollins*Publishers*
77 – 85 Fulham Palace Road
Hammersmith
London
W6 8JB

Browse the complete Collins catalogue at
www.collins.co.uk

© HarperCollins*Publishers* Limited 2014

10 9 8 7 6 5 4 3 2 1

ISBN-13 978 0 00 752197 5

British Library Cataloguing in Publication Data
A Catalogue record for this publication is available from the British Library

Commissioned by Catharine Steers
Project managed by Sue Chapple and Helen Marsden
Production by Emma Roberts
Copy-edited by Philippa Boxer
Development edited by Hugh Hillyard-Parker and Lucy Hobbs
Proofread by Cassie Fox
Indexed by Jane Coulter
Photo research by Shelley Noronha and Lucy Roth
Artwork by Ann Paganuzzi
Concept design by Angela English
Cover design by Angela English
Typeset by Jouve India Private Limited

Printed and bound in China.

Acknowledgements

Every effort has been made to trace copyright holders and to obtain their permission for the use of copyright material. The publishers will gladly receive any information enabling them to rectify any error or omission at the first opportunity. The publishers wish to thank the following for permission to reproduce photographs.

Cover & p 1 Akinso/iStockphoto; p 6 Daniel Allan/Getty; p 14 Andrew Buckin/Shutterstock; p 21 Monkey Business Images/Shutterstock; p 28 Melanie DeFazio/Shutterstock; p 30 Max Topchii/Shutterstock; p 35 Martin Novak/Shutterstock; p 37 Umierov Nariman/Shutterstock; p 41 racorn/Shutterstock; p 48 wavebreakmedia/Shutterstock; p 109 Lisa F. Young/Shutterstock; p 58 Keith Brofsky/Alamy; p 62 CandyBox Images/Shutterstock; p 64 Heritage Images/Getty; p 100 Robert Kneschke/Shutterstock; p 77 Featureflash/Shutterstock; p 92 DreamBig/Shutterstock; p 96 Vlue/Shutterstock; p 113 Rich Legg/Getty; p 115 Will Rodrigues/Shutterstock; p 121 Spencer Platt/Getty; p 124 WaveBreakMedia/Shutterstock; p 125 luckyraccoon/Shutterstock; p 134 WaveBreakMedia/Shutterstock; p 137 Golden Pixels LLC/Shutterstock; p 144 (t) kaarsten/Shutterstock; p 144 (b) Zurijeta/Shutterstock; p 148 Tyler Olson/Shutterstock; p 150 TMCPhotos/Shutterstock; p 152 Science Source/Science Photo Library; p 158 Pressmaster/Shutterstock; p 162 WaveBreakMedia/Shutterstock; p 164 DigitalHand Studio/Shutterstock; p 169 Glenn Hill/Getty; p 170 Gert Vrey/Shutterstock; p 173 Monkey Business Images/Shutterstock; p 177 vesna cvorovic/Shutterstock; p 193 Peter Gudella/Shutterstock; p 203 WaveBreakMedia/Shutterstock.

Contents

Approaches to psychology 2

Approaches: behavioural 4

Approaches: biological. 7

Approaches: cognitive 10

Approaches: evolutionary. 14

Approaches: humanist 19

Approaches: psychodynamic 24

Attachment: formation 30

Attachment: privation & disruption . . 34

Attachment: types 40

Biological rhythms 47

Conditioning: classical 52

Conditioning: operant 57

Conformity 61

Debates: free will & determinism 68

Debates: nature and nurture 72

Disorders: depression 76

Disorders: OCD 84

Disorders: phobias 89

Disorders: schizophrenia 96

Issues: culture and gender bias 100

Issues: reductionism 104

Memory: cognitive interview 108

Memory: eye witness testimony 112

Memory: forgetting 117

Memory: levels of processing 122

Memory: reconstructive 125

Memory: structure 129

Obedience 134

OBEs and NDEs 139

Research: data types 143

Research: design 146

Research: ethics 149

Research: methods. 154

Research: reliability & validity 160

Science & pseudo-science 166

Sleeping: explanations 170

Social learning theory. 176

Stress: bodily responses 181

Stress: individual differences. 185

Stress: workplace. 190

Therapies: behavioural 193

Therapies: biological 198

Therapies: CBT. 203

Therapies: psychoanalysis. 208

Index 215

Dedication 219

Notes. 220

Approaches to psychology

In psychology, there are various ways of looking at the same thing – different points of view or perspectives based on certain assumptions. A psychologist's particular perspective or approach will influence the methods they choose to study both humans and non-humans. It will also influence the type of therapies chosen to treat disorders.

Different approaches in psychology

There are several approaches used in psychology: biological, psychodynamic, behavioural, cognitive, evolutionary and humanistic. Each approach offers reasons why people function as they do, based on a particular set of assumptions.

The different approaches influence the types of methods a psychologist chooses to study phenomena, the conclusions drawn from the studies, and treatments chosen for disorders. These treatments are called therapies, and they may be biological or psychological. To know how each therapy works, you first need to understand the ideas behind the particular approach the therapy is based on.

See also:
Biological approach;
Psychodynamic approach;
Behavioural approach;
Cognitive approach;
Humanist approach;
Evolutionary approach.

How approach affects perception

Langer & Abelson (1974) investigated whether a psychologist's approach would influence their view of a person's behaviour. Clinicians from two psychological approaches (psychodynamic and behavioural) were shown a video of an interview between two men. Half of each group were told the interviewee was a job applicant and the other half were told he was a patient. The researchers expected the psychodynamic clinicians to rate the interviewee as more disturbed than the behaviourist clinicians. They found that the psychodynamic clinicians rated the man as disturbed when told he was a patient, but as relatively normal when told he was an interviewee. In contrast, the behaviourist clinicians rated the man as reasonably well adjusted in both conditions. The researchers suggested the reason for this was that the behaviourists rated the man based only on his overt behaviour, compared to the psychodynamic clinicians who were trained to look further than the surface. As the researchers pointed out, this study was purely to show how approach can affect perception of participants.

Case study: diagnosis and treatment

Jenny is a young woman who feels uncomfortable with strangers, tends to fidget when in company and feels stressed most of the time. Below are examples of how Jenny's issues would be addressed by each form of therapy.

From a *biological* approach, the therapist (e.g. doctor) would first take her symptoms, diagnose her and prescribe a treatment, e.g. a drug.

From a *behavioural* approach, only Jenny's behaviour, or perhaps that of her parents or peers, would be of interest. The behaviourist would not consider Jenny to have a disorder.

From a *psychodynamic* approach, Jenny's childhood would be of interest, as she would be seen as having an unresolved issue in her unconscious.

From a *cognitive* approach, Jenny's thoughts would be of interest, particularly her negative and irrational thoughts. Jenny would probably be classed as having a disorder, as she is unable to cope with her thought processes.

References

LANGER, E. J. & ABELSON, R. P. (1974) A Patient by Any Other Name... Clinician Group Difference in Labelling Bias. *Journal of Consulting and Clinical Psychology*. 42. pp.4–9.

Approaches: behavioural

The behavioural approach focuses on an individual's behaviour when trying to explain any psychological problems they might have. It also helps us to understand how environment might influence how people behave. This approach was the first to carry out investigations on non-humans, as researchers believed their behaviour to be comparable to humans. Using this approach, all behaviour can be explained in terms of learning and the environment.

Learned behaviour

The behavioural approach is also known as learning theory. It starts from the idea that we are born a blank slate, that all our behaviour is learned through our experience with the world and through interaction with others. Behaviourists are only interested in observable behaviour; therefore, if a disorder cannot be seen, it does not exist.

Behaviourists argue that when we have a psychological abnormality, it is due to faulty learning that needs to be corrected. Disorders such as phobias or anxiety disorders are dysfunctional behaviours learned through the processes of classical conditioning, operant conditioning and social learning.

Classical conditioning

When a person learns through association a behavioural psychologist calls this classical conditioning. A stimulus, such as an event in the person's environment, results in a physiological reaction (response), therefore, stimulus and response are linked together.

Watson & Raynor (1920) carried out a study with a young child called Albert. The child was introduced to a series of stimulus items, including a white rat. Initially Albert had no fear of any of the items, including the rat. The child was then subjected to a loud noise every time the rat was present. The loud noise caused Albert distress and, after several trials, Albert became afraid of the rat. This fear was due to the noise becoming associated with the rat. This study demonstrates how a phobia can develop.

See also:
Conditioning:
classical.

Operant conditioning

Learning through direct reward and punishment is known as operant conditioning.

A key researcher in this area was Skinner (1948), who did many studies on a variety of creatures. In one particular study, he conditioned pigeons to become superstitious by using the 'Skinner box' and a series of rewards.
The Skinner box was simply a contraption that a creature would be placed in, where a series of stimuli was present and if the creature made the response that was desirable they would get rewarded. After several rewards, the creature would have to increase the amount of desirable behaviour to get the same reward. Operant conditioning is used frequently in institutions such as prisons and schools.

See also:
Conditioning:
operant.

Social learning theory

According to social learning theory (SLT), we learn through indirect reward. We model ourselves on other people we hold in high regard, such as parents and peers. We then imitate their behaviour, which we see brings rewards, and this makes us feel good (known as vicarious reinforcement).

SLT though does allow for some cognitive ability, as it theorises that when the copied behaviour gets a negative response, a person may rethink whether to continue with that particular behaviour.

The researcher most associated with SLT is Bandura (1961), who produced evidence from his famous 'Bobo doll' study, to show how this form of learning can produce antisocial behaviour, such as physical and verbal aggression.

There is debate over whether social learning theory is a behaviourist theory, as there is a large cognitive element to the theory.

See also: Social
learning theory.

Case study: gambling addiction

Danny is addicted to buying lottery scratch cards and this is becoming a problem, as he cannot afford to buy food, or pay his rent. From a behaviourist point of view, his actions are explained by operant conditioning. Scratch cards offer small wins on quite a frequent basis and Danny is likely to know several people who have also had I wins. Such wins could be seen as a reinforcement, or a reward schedule. Even though Danny does not win often, when he does it strengthens his behaviour, so he continues in the hope he will win the jackpot. This maintains his addiction to buying the cards.

Evaluation of the behavioural approach

As the behavioural approach only concentrates on observed behaviour, it will not class someone as abnormal unless there are overt signs of dysfunctional behaviour, which may avoid possible stigma. The main method of investigation for this approach is by controlled observations, often with laboratory experiments, which allow for a greater level of internal validity in research evidence.

See also: Reductionism.

However, behavioural approaches have been criticised for ignoring the underlying causes of behaviour. They are also criticised for being reductionist, i.e. explaining complex behaviours in very narrow terms.

References

BANDURA, A. et al (1961) Transmission of Aggression Through Imitation of Aggressive Models. *Journal of Abnormal and Social Psychology*. 63. pp.575–82.

SKINNER, B. F. (1948) Superstition in the Pigeon. *Journal of Experimental Psychology*. 38. pp.168–72.

WATSON, J. B. & RAYNOR, R. (1920) Conditioned Emotional Responses. *Journal of Experimental Psychology*. 3. pp.1–14.

See also: Behavioural therapies.

Approaches: biological

The biological approach is based on the assumption that all behaviour is the result of a physical (somatic) cause of some description. There are four biological explanations to focus on: genetic, biochemical, neuro-anatomical (brain structure) and micro-organisms (infection). Research evidence from this approach is generally produced using quantitative methods, most commonly via laboratory experiments and correlations that use physiological tests to measure one or more variables, for example, the studies by Kiecolt-Glaser into the effects of stress on the immune system, due to stress hormone secretion.

Genetic explanations

These focus on whether a person may have inherited a particular gene from their parent(s) that may manifest a behaviour such as aggression or a mental illness. This tendency towards a behaviour or condition is called a predisposition, in other words the person is more vulnerable to developing a behaviour than the general population.

Research into possible genetic causes of behaviour uses twin, adoption and family studies, looking at how frequently a behaviour occurs among relatives depending on their genetic relatedness. Results of these investigations will show concordance rates (occurrence rates). Genes can also explain the presence of a biochemical imbalance or an abnormality in a person's brain structure.

Evaluation

➤ The theory can be scientifically tested, therefore creating reliable and valid research evidence.

➤ A problem is the lack of 100% concordance rates, which suggests other reasons for behaviour besides inheritence.

Biochemical explanations

These suggest behaviour is due to the interaction of neuro-transmitters and hormones (the endocrine system) within the nervous system. For example, the sleep cycle can be affected by a biochemical imbalance during the winter, when the hours of darkness are at their longest; there will be an increased secretion of melatonin, causing drowsiness. The excessive release of this hormone will trigger a chain reaction, as levels of serotonin, which produces melatonin and is one of the most important neurotransmitters in the body, will become depleted. This will then affect mood, which could lead to seasonal affective disorder (SAD).

Evaluation

➤ Drug therapy in many disorders has been shown to be effective e.g. HRT Is a therapy given to women of menopausal age to replace lost hormones, which has a significant effect on both psychological and physical health.

➤ Not all drugs work the same for all people with a given condition, therefore there must be more involved than biochemical factors.

Neuro-anatomical explanations

Brain structure anomalies (irregularities) explain disorders in terms of specific areas of the brain that may be abnormal; for example, it is thought that the parts of the brain responsible for language are the Wernicke's (controls comprehension of speech) and Broca's (controls production of speech) areas. These areas are in the cerebral cortex and are named after the psychologists who identified and developed theory on them. The problem with this explanation is identifying which came first: the structural abnormality (causing the mental illness) or the illness (causing structural abnormality).

Micro-organisms explanation

The micro-organisms or infection explanation of psychopathology is the only biological explanation not linked to a person's genes, as it describes a biological cause from infection by pathogens, such as viruses and bacteria. The effect of infection can be severe and lead to psychological instability. For example, the sexually-transmitted infection syphilis is well known for its effect on mental health.

A problem with this explanation is that many people may come into contact with a bacterial or viral infection, but not all will be affected in the same way. For example, if a person has an unhealthy diet, their immune system becomes depleted, leading to a higher vulnerability to infection. Therefore, environment must play a part.

Case study: schizophrenia

A psychological disorder that is linked with all four biological explanations is schizophrenia. For example, Gottesman (1991) found a lifetime risk of developing schizophrenia of 48% if the person had an identical twin with the disorder and a risk of up to 46% if both parents had the disorder.

Infection is also implicated. Torrey et al (1996) found a higher-than-normal occurrence of schizophrenia in people born in the winter; this links with a study that found the viral infection of influenza A in the mother during pregnancy often led to a diagnosis of schizophrenia later for that child.

References

GOTTESMAN, I. (1991) *Schizophrenia Genesis: The Origins Of Madness*. New York: Freeman.

TORREY, E. F. et al (1996) Birth Seasonality in Bipolar Disorder, Schizophrenia, Schizoaffective Disorder and Stillbirths. *Schizophrenia Research*. 21 (3). pp.141–9.

Approaches: cognitive

The cognitive approach is extremely diverse, incorporating: attention, learning, memory, language, emotion, IQ and thinking. Also known as the information-processing approach, there is an analogy between the mind and computers. Major names in the field include Chomsky and his theory of language, Broadbent and his theory of attention, and Miller with his theory of magic number 7 in short-term memory. Ellis revolutionised psychotherapy with his book *Reason and Emotion in Psychotherapy*.

The role of mental processes

This approach proposes that the mind is like a computer: processing information according to complex sets of data derived from a wide variety of sources. These sources are diverse in nature, from genetic to social, and are sustained by a complex array of monitoring and feedback capacity. In other words, this approach does not restrict its view, but deals with all information from whatever source available.

The approach then embraces and is incorporated into other approaches, such as the cognitive-behavioural approach and social learning theory. Its influence is also felt in areas of social cognition such as perception, attribution and attitudes such as prejudice.

Basic principles

The cognitive approach attempts to describe the as-yet unexplained workings of the human brain using an array of familiar metaphors and analogies. The analogy with a computer information processing system offers features such as coding, capacity, serial and parallel processing. Some of these features appear in a variety of topics. In the topic of memory, two of the main models (the multi-store model by Atkinson & Shiffrin and the working memory model by Baddeley and Hitch) use such terms as encoding and capacity, along with how memory is processed.

See also: Memory: structure.

This approach generally uses experimental methods of investigation and which involve a diverse range of technical equipment, such as; Positron Emission tomography (PET) scans, which show detailed images of brain activity. This approach may also use case studies, when there are unusual cases i.e. with amnesia cases, but the investigations will remain quantitative for the case study.

Beck's cognitive triad

Beck devised his cognitive triad to explain depression. In the cognitive triad he described three forms of negative thinking.

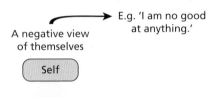

E.g. 'I am no good at anything.'

A negative view of themselves

Self

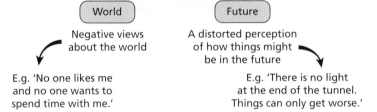

World

Negative views about the world

E.g. 'No one likes me and no one wants to spend time with me.'

Future

A distorted perception of how things might be in the future

E.g. 'There is no light at the end of the tunnel. Things can only get worse.'

Cognitive distortions

Beck (1967) suggested that negative self-schemas could start in childhood as a result of a number of reasons, such as death of a parent, bullying or parental rejection. When that person encounters a situation resembling their past experience, the negative self-schemas come to mind. These bring self-doubt, caused by logical errors in their thinking. Beck called these errors 'cognitive distortions'.

Examples of different types of cognitive distortions can be found in the following table.

Cognitive distortions	Thinking process	Example
Arbitrary inference	Drawing conclusions about yourself based on evidence that does not relate to you.	The rain pours down on a bride's wedding day; she concludes she is useless at planning things.
Selective abstractions	Seeing only one tiny aspect of a situation and ignoring the big picture.	A teacher feels it is their fault if a student fails an exam, ignoring the fact that most of the class passed.
Overgeneralisation	Drawing conclusions based on isolated events.	A student gets an E grade, instead of her usual B grade, and concludes she is not intelligent enough to achieve her goals.
Magnification and minimisation	Exaggerating or underplaying events.	A graduate who gains three degrees feels a failure because none of them is at the grade he wanted.
Personalisation	Assuming that other people's negative feelings must be toward them.	Jessica's boss comes into work in a bad mood. Jessica assumes she must have done something wrong; it must be her fault.

Transactional model of stress

An example of the cognitive approach to psychopathology is the transactional model of stress (Lazarus & Folkman 1984) which suggests different people perceive a stressor in very different ways. This then has an impact on the way they perceive their ability to cope with it. For example, a person with a fear of spiders may see a spider as a deadly tarantula instead of a harmless bug and will feel unable to cope.

Evaluation of the cognitive approach

The cognitive approach is very popular in modern psychology.

Strengths

➤ It takes a scientific approach and its theories lend themselves to scientific testing.

➤ The fact that it is so diverse in its scope means it may achieve what no other approach has achieved – amalgamating psychology within one paradigm (idea), which will bring it closer to being accepted by all as a bona fide science.

Weaknesses

➤ The approach is still relatively new and has a tendency to vagueness as to how the information processes operate: more description than substance.

➤ There is some ambiguity relating to the cause of the disorder: do irrational thinking and negative thoughts *cause* psychological disorders, or are they a result of them?

➤ The individual is seen as responsible for their thoughts and behaviour, so downplaying other factors such as difficulties in the environment or biological causes.

Therapies based on a cognitive approach

This approach led to the development of various therapies, grouped under the category of cognitive-behavioural therapy (CBT). This encourages people to replace irrational, negative thoughts with a more rational, positive way of thinking. CBT includes both a cognitive element (thinking about beliefs) and a behavioural element (setting goals for changing behaviour).

See also:
Therapies: CBT.

References

BECK, A. T. (1963) Thinking and Depression. *Archives of General Psychiatry*. 9. pp.324–33.

BECK, A. T. (1967) *Depression: Clinical Experimental and Theoretical Aspects*. New York: Harper and Row.

LAZARUS, R. S. & FOLKMAN, S. (1984). *Stress, Appraisal and Coping*. New York: Springer.

Approaches: evolutionary

The evolutionary approach is greatly influenced by Darwin (1859). Its core idea is that how we think, feel and behave is related to hereditary factors that have been the key to our survival. It suggests those who can adapt to their environment most easily are most likely to survive. Evolution theory is linked to biological psychology due to genetic influence, but is also thought by some to provide a unity to all areas of psychology, in the same way it has united biology.

Theory of evolution

Darwin's theory of evolution suggested that a species, such as humans, originates out of a common species ancestry. Over a period of time, there will be a break away from the common ancestry and a unique species will form. This new species will be similar to the original common species type, but will be different enough that reproduction with the former species is not possible. This process is thought to be due to genetic variation. Darwin identified several key principles of this process.

Natural selection

This is a key mechanism of the evolutionary theory. It is a gradual process whereby biological traits become more or less common depending on several factors, such as if the traits will improve chances of reproducing the species. If the trait is desirable, it will become more common, as the animal with that trait will have greater opportunity to mate and reproduce. A less fortunate trait, such as being an albino peacock, will mean there is less chance of reproducing, as it becomes easy prey.

Variation in population

A person's characteristics are determined by their DNA, which is part of their genome. Variation occurs as a result of random mutation of the genome. This mutation will be passed on to offspring, and interaction with the environment – diet, education, etc – will cause further variation. Natural selection then acts as a phenotype (observable characteristic), which may become more common and eventually emerge as a new species. Natural selection is a precursor to the theory of genetics, therefore genetic explanations of behaviour have derived originally from the theory of evolution's natural selection.

Types of selection

Types of selection that are of most interest to psychologists are competition, which is ecological selection, and sexual selection. Competition can be direct or indirect and is about hoarding and distribution of resources that enable that species to control resources and territory. Sexual selection determines who parents the next generation, so whose traits will live on and multiply.

Ecological selection – competition

There are several types of competition, one of which is interference competition, which is a direct form of competition between individuals in their fight for resources to enable the greatest capacity for survival and ultimately the greatest chance of reproducing. This is often called 'survival of the fittest'.

Sexual selection

This features in the evolutionary explanation of relationships and aggression. There are two types: intra-sexual and inter-sexual selection.

Intra-sexual selection is where one gender competes for mates of the opposite gender. Traits such as strength and dominance are useful, as rivals can be overpowered, so allowing more abundant reproduction. For example, if strong men are more likely to get the chance to reproduce than men who are small and weak, the traits of height and muscular build will become more common. This is evidenced by the average height in the human population generally increasing with each generation. Men who are more aggressive are more likely to overpower rivals, so the aggressive gene will be another trait that continues.

Inter-sexual selection is where one gender (usually female) chooses whom to mate with. This is an example of the difference between male and female behaviour in romantic relationships, which is thought to be due to sex difference, where the female has a gestation period of 9 months to reproduce in comparison to a male who only has to be there for as long as it takes to mate. The man is looking for quantity and the woman quality of partner (resources).

Research
Key psychologists in the area of sexual selection are Trivers with his theory of parental and sexual selection (1972), which showed women evolve with preference for mates who seem more willing to contribute resources to their offspring. He also went on to suggest the gender that invests more in their offspring (generally the female) will be more choosy when selecting a partner.

David Buss is another evolutionary psychologist who has been influential in relationship psychology with studies looking at mate preferences in sexual selection. Buss and Schmitt 1993 conducted a task analysis on adaptive problems of both genders in both short and long term relationships.

Evolution of the mind – development of intelligence

Many Evolutionary Psychologists argue that it is necessary to understand how the environment has impacted on brain evolution, to allow us to truly understand how the brain works, this is identified as the Environment of Evolutionary Adaptiveness (EEA). The EEA idea was first used effectively in John Bowlby's attachment theory, which explains how the environment evolved particular mechanisms, such as social releasers.

See also:
Attachment:
formation.

It is suggested EEA began around 10,000 to 2 million years ago. This allowed humans to adapt, in order to solve the problems of the environment e.g. foraging (seeking food) or avoiding predators, those adapting most effecting, as those that survived to pass on the genes.

Application
The EEA theory can help explain modern society's problems with obesity. In our evolutionary past, food was scarce and seasonal, so humans had a natural need for fatty foods. Fat provided the most energy and was easy for the body to store. Although food is now readily available, the desire for fatty food that provides storage of energy resources still remains. Responding to this desire leads to obesity in an increasingly overweight population.

Common evolutionary psychology research practice is to study the behaviour of non-humans, such as Konrad Lorenz with his theory of imprinting, which impacted on Bowlby's 'sensitive period' (cross ref to evolutionary formation of attachment). Due to the lack of human hunter-gatherer societies, EP's often look at our closest relatives in the animal world i.e. chimps. Ryan and Jetha (2010) find a problem with the favoured chimps in research, as they are more violent than humans may have been in the past and suggest bonobos are a much more appropriate species when comparing human temperament.

Evaluation of evolutionary approach
One of the main criticisms of evolutionary pyschology is that much of the theory is not falsifiable, due to the fact that assumptions are made about the past, for example theories about adaptation to environment are to a large

part guess work. This criticism is answered by asserting there is a knowledge of past conditions in the environment, for example that society was hunter-gatherer based and females were the gender becoming pregnant. Even given this, though perhaps not enough detail is known about who our ancestors were and what they had to face.

Altruism and kin selection

An evolutionary explanation for altruism suggests that those of the same species will help each other out in order to ensure the survival of the species as a whole. More recently, the idea of 'meme' has developed. This suggests that particular cultural behaviour, such as altruism, spreads from one mind to another and passes on from one generation to the next, in the same way as genes pass on physiologically (Dawkins 1989).

Altruism extends to kin selection, which is an evolutionary strategy to ensure reproductive success and survival of closely related organisms. In humans, the closer the relation the more likely they are to be helped, which in turn improves their chances of genetic success. This is called inclusive fitness. This is achieved through altruistic social behaviour, for example when a woman is unable to reproduce a close relative, such as a mother or sister, may volunteer to be a surrogate mother.

References

DARWIN, C. (1859) On the Origin of Species by Means of Natural Selection, or the Preservation of Favoured Races in the Struggle for Life. *Nature*. 5 (121) 502.

DAWKINS, R. (1989) *The Selfish Gene*. 2nd Ed. Oxford: Oxford University Press.

KALAT, J. W. (2004) *Biological Psychology*. London: Thomson.

RYAN, C. & JETHÁ, C. (2010) *Sex at Dawn: The Prehistoric Origins of Modern Sexuality*. Harper.

Approaches: humanist

This approach was founded on the ideas of two key psychologists: Maslow with his 'theory of human motivation' (1943) and Roger's (1951) idea that troubled people had their own answers within them. The therapist's role was to provide the key to open the lock. Humanism represented a move away from a scientific approach, favouring case studies instead of experimentation. It was based on a belief that there is good in everyone; they just need help to develop their sense of self.

Principles of the humanist approach

Bugental (1967), the first president of the American Association for Humanistic Psychology, put forward the main principles of the humanistic approach:

➤ A proper understanding of human nature can only be gained from studying humans, not other animals.

➤ Psychology should research areas that are meaningful and important to human existence, not neglect them because they are too difficult.

➤ Psychology should study internal experience as well as external behaviour and consider that individuals can show some degree of free will.

➤ Psychology should study the individual case (an idiographic method) rather than the average performance of groups (a nomothetic approach).

➤ In general, humanistic psychologists assume that the whole person should be studied in their environment.

Maslow's hierarchy of human needs

Maslow's view of people was that they are innately good and capable. In his book *Motivation and Personality* (1945), he explains how an individual has to progress through a structure of needs that must be built upon, like a pyramid.

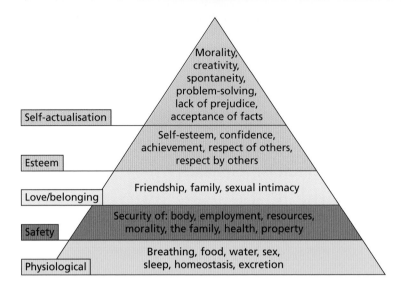

Maslow saw the hierarchy as a starting point for individual development. He suggested that people need to meet all their base needs before they could reach self-actualisation and have a meaningful life.

Once people have reached self-actualisation, they are compelled to keep working towards their full potential through a process of growth motivation or 'metamotivation' (Maslow 1967). Mental illness occurs when 'metaneeds', such as autonomy and meaningfulness are not met, and so people do not work toward fulfilling their potential. This can be due to factors such as: upbringing; lack of education; anxiety; and fear, including an inner fear of success (the so-called 'Jonah complex').

Rogers' client-centred therapy

Following on from Maslow's ideas, Rogers developed a form of psychotherapy called 'client-centred therapy' (CCT), more recently known as person-centred therapy (PCT). The main aims of this therapy were to:

➤ Build or develop a positive self-regard in the client

➤ Help people with the process of reaching self-actualisation and beyond

➤ Help people gain insight into how their attitudes, feelings and actions can be negatively affected by not understanding who they are

➤ Help people to become 'whole' and therefore able to accept all aspects of self, an idea based on Gestalt therapy (Fritz et al 1951).

In order to achieve these aims, Rogers gave the following guidelines for therapists:

➤ Provide a comfortable, non-judgemental environment

➤ Develop and use skills of empathy

➤ Have an attitude of unconditional positive regard (only treating the person in a positive way)

➤ Use a non-directive approach (i.e. not leading or questioning the client, but allowing them to express themselves freely and helping them to find their own answers).

Key humanist method: Q-sort method

Stephenson (1953) developed the Q-sort method, which Rogers later used to help in assessing a client's progress. The client is given a bundle of 100 cards, each having a statement on such as 'Very outgoing and social'. The client reads each statement aloud and places the cards in a nine-point continuum, ranging from 'very much like' to 'very much not like'. First they do this exercise as their 'real self' and then as their 'ideal self'. The closer the results of real and ideal self, the more mentally healthy the person is.

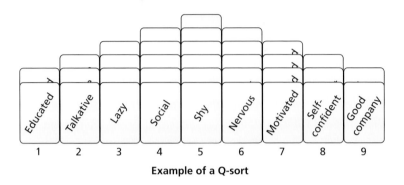

Example of a Q-sort

Evaluation of the humanist approach

Advantages

➤ It looks at *the whole person*, rather than reducing human behaviour or comparing human behaviour to that of animals.

➤ It is a useful alternative to the psychodynamic approach, which can be seen as negatively deterministic, and the behaviourist approach, which views human behaviour as a result of stimulus and response.

➤ It champions idiographic methods when looking at personality and abnormality. Rogers' way of measuring the effectiveness of psychotherapy (Q-sort method), is now used by psychotherapists from other approaches.

➤ It stresses that all people have free will and therefore freedom of choice.

Drawbacks

➤ Because of its rejection of the nomothetic approach, it never gained mainstream credibility.

➤ As most evidence about the humanistic approach lacks empiricism and objective study, it is not possible to generalise or predict behaviour. This goes against psychology's assertion of being a science.

Case study: diagnosis and treatment

Tim is very stressed and quite depressed with his work. This is affecting other areas of his life, such as his relationships. He feels he is doing badly at work and has been overlooked for training and promotion, but is afraid to talk openly with his manager. He thinks he should be able to afford holidays, a nice house and car as other people his age can.

From the humanist approach, Tim's problems are due to him comparing himself to others and his concern with what society sees as 'success'. He needs to discover who *he* is and what will make him happy. By finding himself he will feel less pressure to attain what he thinks society demands of him.

References

BUGENTAL, J. (1964) The Third Force in Psychology. *Journal of Humanistic Psychology*. 4(1). pp.19–26.

BUGENTAL, J. F. T. (ed.) (1967) *Challenges of Humanistic Psychology*. New York, NY: McGraw-Hill.

MASLOW, A. H. (1943) A Theory of Human Motivation. *Psychological Review*. 50 (4). pp.370–96.

MASLOW, A. H. (1954) *Motivation and Personality*. New York Harper.

MASLOW, A. H. (1967) A Theory of Metamotivation: The Biological Rooting of the Value-Life. *Journal of Humanistic Psychology*. 7 (2). pp.93–127.

ROGERS, CARL. (1951) *Client-Centered Therapy*. Cambridge, MA: The Riverside Press.

ROGERS, C. (1957) The Necessary and Sufficient Conditions of Therapeutic Personality Change. *Journal of Consulting Psychology*. 21 (2). pp.95–103.

ROGERS, C. et al (2013) *On Becoming an Effective Teacher – Person-Centered Teaching, Psychology, Philosophy, and Dialogues with Carl R. Rogers and Harold Lyon*. London: Routledge.

STEPHENSON, W. (1953) *The Study of Behavior: Q-technique and Its Methodology*. Chicago: University of Chicago Press.

Approaches: psychodynamic

This theory, developed by Sigmund Freud in the early 20th century, says that personality is shaped by childhood experience. Children have specific needs during different developmental stages and, if these are not met, unresolved conflicts (fixations) may have psychological impact throughout adult life. This approach introduced the idea of the unconscious mind, filled with these unresolved conflicts, and causing negative emotions to surface. Without psychoanalysis these conflicts cannot be accessed and addressed.

Levels of consciousness

According to Freud, there are three different levels of consciousness. Conscious state is where there is full awareness of the present, such as perception, feelings and thoughts. Pre-conscious is information that is just out of reach, such as long term memory, so the information is only accessible if called upon. Unconsciousness is where the content/information is inaccessible to the conscious mind. It also contains the person's unconscious motivations, which may come to the conscious mind via dreams.

See also:
Memory:
forgetting.

Instincts and desires

Freud suggested that people are born with instincts, needs and desires ranging from nourishment to sex and aggression. He further suggested that these desires motivated the needs for love, knowledge and security. However, the task of having desires met is frustrated by outside influences, such as social pressures. The characteristics of an adult's personality are shaped by the outcome of their struggles to have their basic instinctual needs met in childhood.

Theory of personality, or theory of mind

In Freud's theory of personality, the id, ego and superego act in different levels of consciousness. There is also movement between the differing levels of consciousness e.g. emotions, impulses, drives will move through the different levels.

Id – We are born with id, which resides in the unconscious and is our life force (libido). It operates on the pleasure principle: it seeks instant gratification and is therefore impulsive. There are two impulses or drives in id: *eros* (sex), which is positive and constructive, and *thanatos*, responsible for aggression and destructiveness (Hall et al. 1998).

Ego – As society places restrictions on the impulses of id, ego is developed. Ego works on the reality principle: it tries to get what a person wants in the real world, refereeing the impulses of id with the constraints of the real world and the desires of Superego.

Superego – As a person internalises the rules and values of society, superego develops. This works on the morality principle: it tells the person what they should and shouldn't do.

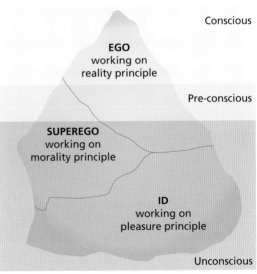

The iceberg representation of the human mind

Defence mechanisms

The ego protects itself with defence mechanisms, which help it to function. In people without a disorder, defence mechanisms effectively maintain an everyday level of function, keeping distressing issues from intruding in their conscious mind. Common ego defence mechanisms are:

➤ Denial – refusing to accept that a problem exists (e.g. an alcoholic saying 'I could stop drinking any time if I wanted')

➤ Sublimation – diverting emotion into another area (e.g. releasing anger through aggressive sport)

➤ Projection – attributing our own feelings or wishes to someone else (e.g. accusing someone of being unreasonable when it is you who is being unreasonable)

➤ Repression – forcing unwanted behaviours, desires or emotions into the unconscious (e.g. acting violently but having no memory of it).

Psychosexual stages of development

Freud suggested that a person's personality develops during five psychosexual stages of development (see table). As we move from infancy to adulthood, different parts of the body will be the focus of the id's constant pleasure-seeking. In each stage the needs of the child have to be met appropriately, or there will be unresolved conflicts and problems in the unconscious – known as fixation.

Fixation generally only happens in the first three stages of development, but its effects can lead to life-long problems. The aim of psychoanalysis is to resolve any fixations.

	Stage of development	Focus of development
1	Oral stage (0–18 months)	Pleasure gained, for example, from eating and sucking. Child is weaned.
2	Anal stage (18–36 months)	Pleasure gained from expelling or retaining faeces. Child learns bladder and bowel control.
3	Phallic stage (3–6 years)	The child becomes aware of gender and focusses on the genitals. Passing through this stage successfully requires the development of a firm gender identity.
4	Latency stage (6 years to puberty)	The focus is on social rather than psychosexual development.
5	Genital stage (puberty to maturity)	If earlier conflicts are resolved, pleasure comes from mature (hetero)sexual relationships.

Later psychodynamic theorists generally agree that experiences that happen after these developmental stages can cause unresolved conflicts.

Oedipus complex

Freud suggested boys around the ages of 3–5 years want to possess their mothers sexually and see their father as competition for her. Their urge is to eliminate the father (this is unacceptable to the ego, so thoughts have to be repressed). At the same time the boy will fear his father, because he is frightened his father will castrate him. All this causes a conflict. In order to resolve the conflict, the boy will be driven by the ego to identify with his father, e.g. imitating his behaviour, helping out with 'male chores' or watching male sports together. In this way, the fear can be dispelled and the conflict resolved.

Electra complex

There are differing interpretations about girls in the phallic stage. One theory suggests that a girl has a strong attachment to her mother on entering this stage, but then realises she does not have a penis and so develops 'penis envy'. She transfers her love to the father, which is known as the 'Electra complex'. So as not to lose her mother's love and affection, she identifies with her and imitates her, e.g. by carrying out 'female chores' and playing with 'girl toys'. This allows her to go on and develop her superego.

Research: Little Hans

With this approach, the most common research method is the case study, as the theory is primarily interested in the complexity of the human condition. Case studies can incorporate interviews and questionnaires, there can also be series of case studies that are connected by commonality of experience, such as child abuse. They may also be part of a government-funded programme, such as health promotion. Surveys, longitudinal and correlation studies are also used.

See also:
Research
methods.

Freud's theory was built on case studies of patients, both his own and those of others he worked with, such as Breuer and Jung.

In one such case study, Little Hans presented with a terrible fear of horses. His fear was explained using the phallic stage of the psychosexual stages of development. Freud suggested that the boy had unresolved issues in the form of an Oedipus complex, a fear of being castrated by his father, because of his unconscious desire for his mother. Freud rationalised that Hans had transferred his fear of his father (who had a beard and wore eye glasses) to his horse (which had long whiskers and wore blinkers). The horse therefore represented the father.

Influence of the psychodynamic approach

Freud's psychodynamic theory has proved highly influential and has had a huge impact on the way we think about what motivates behaviour. It also led to the development of 'talking therapies'. Though the psychodynamic approach lost a great deal of credibility and went out of fashion in the 1970s and 1980s, it has once again emerged as an important approach, with such treatments as transactional analysis, inter-personal psychotherapy and play therapy. It has now transcended from a purely psychodynamic approach and makes a very important contribution in helping children develop into healthy-minded individuals.

See also:
Therapies:
psychoanalysis.

Criticisms of the psychodynamic approach

➤ These theories have been accused of not being scientific, as they were developed from Freud's case studies, not scientific data. Hence, they are difficult to test scientifically.

➤ Case histories often rely on recalling events from past – which might make them unreliable. This means they also tend to downplay current experiences.

References

FREUD, S. (1917) Introductory Lectures on Psychoanalysis. I. STRACHEY, J. (ed.) The Complete Works of Sigmund Freud, Vol 16. New York: Norton.

HALL, C. S. et al (1998) Theories of Personality. 4th Ed. New York: Wiley.

Attachment: formation

The evolutionary theory of formation of attachment was proposed by Bowlby (1951), who believed that forming a strong first attachment was essential to give infants the best possible chance of survival. He referred to the mother but it is generally agreed that, as long as the child forms a healthy and sustained attachment to a primary carer, whoever that maybe, the child will have the best chances of normal development.

Adaptive behaviour and social releasers

According to Bowlby, humans have evolved so that infants are born to display adaptive behaviour, i.e. behaviour that helps secure their survival. This behaviour is innate. They use social releasers, which are social behaviours designed to attract attention and elicit a care-giving response, such as crying or smiling. The mother or main carer will respond intuitively to these releasers and repeatedly meet the child's emotional and physical needs, so creating a bond with the child. Bowlby also suggested that emotional comfort was more vital than the basic need of food in the formation of attachment. They are born with social releasers, which are innate behaviours.

The monotropic bond

Through the mother's constant response to the child, eventually a monotropic bond (the first bond of a child's life, said to be the most important one-to-one bond they will make) is formed. The strength and quality of this bond affects the child's social, cognitive, emotional and physical development.

The bond also creates an internal working model – a template for all future relationships and a guide for the child of how to form attachments and interact with others in society.

Sensitive (critical) period

This monotropic bond has to be formed within the first two years of a child's life. This is known as the sensitive, or critical, period. Bowlby felt if a child did not make their monotropic bond within this time, their social, cognitive, emotional and physical development could become negatively affected. More recent research has shown that the bond is best formed within the first seven months of a child's life for the best future outcome.

The notion of a sensitive period comes from Bowlby's knowledge of the work of Konrad Lorenz (1935). Lorenz studied the importance of a hatched bird's first experiences. He found that birds will follow the first moving object they see to ensure their survival. This was called 'imprinting' and had a very brief critical period of time, within the first few moments after hatching.

In Schaffer and Emerson's (1964) longitudinal study on Glaswegian infants, the forming of a special bond with the mother was evident between 6–9 months in most children. As a result of the research, they created their theory of phases of attachment, with bond-forming taking place in the 'discriminate phase'.

When the child is around 9 months old and has secured the monotropic bond with the main care giver, it will progress to the multiple attachment phase, where strong additional bonds are formed, firstly with other major care givers and then with their widening social circle.

Case study: child development

The New Orleans intervention/Tulane infant team created by Larrieu & Zeanah (1998) works with fostered children under 5 who have previously been treated badly. Their health and developments are met using a multi-disciplinary team, specialising in child development and psychopathology. A primary goal is to encourage and support the development of an attachment to their foster carer, as research shows a marked improvement in the quality of a child's development when there is a good bond formed between the child and foster carer. The intervention used is the ABC programme (Attachment and Biobehavioural Catchup). This has four main parts which train the foster carer to nurture the child effectively. This is a new intervention, but the results appear promising. (Dozier & Rutter, 2008)

Evaluation

Bowlby's theory is supported by research.

➤ A study by Harlow & Zimmerman (1958) took rhesus monkeys from their mothers at birth and tested if food or comfort was more important when forming an attachment to a surrogate. The surrogate was either a model of a monkey made of wire which had a bottle containing milk, or a model of a monkey with a cloth covering for comfort. The monkeys spent most of their time on the cloth monkey, only going to the wire monkey when hungry. This study supported Bowlby's idea that comfort was more important than food. Food was thought to be the primary reason for attachment from the behaviourist approach.

➤ The Schaffer and Emerson study (1964) also supported Bowlby's idea that a child needs to form a particular bond with the main carer, before they go on to form attachments to others.

➤ Research that questions Bowlby's assertions include Kagen (1984), which said it was more likely to be the child's personality (temperament) that determined the type of response a child had to the primary care-giver and in turn this would determine if a healthy bond was formed, rather than Bowlby's idea that babies and mothers are all instinctively programmed. Support for Kagen's ideas was gained from Spangler (1990), who found via a study of German mothers that a perception of their child's temperament did influence their responsiveness.

References

BOWLBY, J. (1951) *Maternal Care and Mental Health*. Geneva: World Health Organisation.

BOWLBY, J. et al (1956) The Effects of Mother–Child Separation: A Follow-Up Study. *British Journal of Medical Psychology*. 29. p.211.

DOZIER, M. & RUTTER, M. (2008). Challenges to the Development of Attachment Relationships Faced by Young Children in Foster and Adoptive Care. In CASSIDY, J. & Shaver, P. R. *Handbook of Attachment: Theory, Research and Clinical Applications*. 2nd Ed. New York: London: Guilford Press.

HARLOW, H. F. & ZIMMERMANN, R. R. (1958) The development of Affective Responsiveness in Infant Monkeys. *Proceedings of the American Philosophical Society*. 102. pp.501–9.

KAGAN, J. et al (1978) Infancy - Its Place in Human Development. Cambridge MA: Harvard University Press.

LARRIEU, J. A., & ZEANAH, C. H. (2004). Treating Infant-Parent Relationships In the context of Maltreatment: An Integrated, Systems Approach. In SANER, A., McDonagh, S. & Roesenblaum, K. (Eds.) *Treating Parent-Infant Relationship Problems*. 243–264. New York: Guilford Press.

LORENZ, K. Z. (1935) The Companion in the Bird's World. *Auk*. 54. pp.245–73.

SCHAFFER, H. R. & EMERSON, P. E. (1964) The Development of Social Attachments in Infancy. *Monographs of the Society for Research in Child Development*. 29 (Whole No. 3).

SPANGLER, G. (October–December 1990) Mother, Child, and Situational Correlates of Toddlers' Social Competence. *Infant Behavior and Development*. 13 (4). pp.405–19.

SROUFE, L. A. et al (2005) The Development of the Person: The Minnesota Study of Risk and Adaptation from Birth to Adulthood. New York: Guilford.

Bowlby believed that a child who cannot form a monotropic bond by the end of the sensitive period, or who has the bond disrupted in either the long or short term, will suffer from delayed development. Development psychologists later separated disruption and lack of the initial bond by considering the effects of separation, deprivation and privation.

Key researchers

Researchers have investigated the effects of disruption and privation in attachment, and whether these effects are permanent or can be reversed. The table summarises these concepts and some of the key pieces of research.

	Description	Research
Separation	When a child has formed an attachment to their main care-giver, but there are brief periods of being apart, e.g. when a child goes to nursery.	Robertson & Robertson (1969): 'Young children in brief separation'
Deprivation	When a child has formed an attachment, but there are either long periods of discontinuity or it is a dysfunctional attachment.	Bowlby (1944): 'Forty-four juvenile thieves'
Privation	When a child has no opportunity of forming an attachment owing to isolation or neglect.	Hodges & Tizard (1989): 'Teenagers raised in orphanages' Case studies: Genie (Curtis 1977), Czech twins (Koluchová 1976)

Effects of disruption and privation

See also:
Attachment:
types.

Researchers have found that separation, disruption and privation can have negative cognitive, emotional, social and physical effects. Privation seems to have the most severe consequences, for example in the case study by Curtiss of Genie, a teenage girl who had never had a chance to form an attachment. Genie had been socially isolated and deprived of the most basic care and was found in a severe state:

➤ cognitively (lacking In language ability),

➤ emotionally (was generally lacking in normal overt emotion),

➤ socially (had very poor social skills, e.g. could not interact in conversation vocally)

➤ physically (being excessively small for her age, and barely able to walk through a combination of poor nourishment and rickets)

A study by Quinton et al (1985) studied the long-term effects of institutional care, comparing 50 women raised from birth in children's homes (experimental group) with 50 woman brought up with parents (control group). They were all in their 20s and it was found many of those brought up in institutions lacked emotional warmth when interacting with their own children and found parenting extremely difficult.

Maternal deprivation hypothesis (MDH)

The maternal deprivation hypothesis (MDH) was developed by John Bowlby (1951). Bowlby believed a child needed to 'experience a warm, intimate and continuous relationship with his mother (or permanent mother-figure) in which both find satisfaction'. If deprived of a healthy attachment to the mother, the child will suffer severely delayed or lack of development in:

➤ cognitive development – the child's academic and reasoning abilities would be affected

➤ emotional development – the child would have difficulty dealing with their emotions, which could lead to psychopathology

➤ social development – ranging from antisocial behaviour through to becoming an affectionless psychopath (someone with no respect for self or others, lacking in emotional sensitivity and likely to turn to crime)

➤ physical development – a child's physical growth may be affected by an interruption in the monotropic bond.

Research: Bowlby's 'Forty-four juvenile thieves' (1944)
Bowlby theorised that early separation of the main attachment figure (mother) would lead to problems in the child's development later in life. He had noticed in his clinical work many of his worst cases had experienced such separation. Early separation is classed as separation happening before the child reaches 2 years.

All his participants were children aged 5 to 16 who had been referred to his clinic for dysfunctional behaviour. He formed two groups of 44. One group (experimental group) were known thieves and the other was not known to be thieves (control group). Prior to the study Bowlby had diagnosed 14 of the thieves as affectionless psychopaths. The study consisted of interviews with the children and their parents, which included early life experiences.

Bowlby found that of the juvenile thieves classed as affectionless psychopaths, 86% (12 out of 14) had early separation, while 17% (5 out of 30) of the other thieves had early separation (an average of 39% for all the thieves). In the control group, only 4% (two out of 44) had early separation. The conclusion was that lack of continuous care could ultimately lead to affectionless psychopaths.

Bowlby's study has certain limitations:

➤ This study involved correlation, which does not show cause and effect. It is therefore incorrect to assume that early separation causes a child to become an affectionless psychopath

➤ There is a problem with how the data was collected, as parents had to answer questions retrospectively (from past memory) and they could have been subject to social desirability bias (answering in a way that made them look good to the researcher)

➤ Bowlby's diagnoses may have been biased, as his participants were his patients so he already had a pre-determined judgement of them.

Reactive attachment disorder

A rare condition that can develop from disruption or lack of proper attachment in early years is reactive attachment disorder (RAD). This is where the child has learnt the world is an unsafe place and adults cannot be trusted or relied on. There are thought to be two forms of the disorder: inhibited and disinhibited. With the inhibited type, the person is unable to initiate or respond successfully to social interaction, which leads to lack of appropriate development. The disinhibited type is overly familiar with everyone, including strangers. The disinhibited form is often referred to as DAD.

Though two distinct types have been identified, the DSM V (Charles & Gleason, 2010) refers to them as one disorder (RAD), as both derive from the failure to form a normal attachment with a primary care giver, which results in the lack of a healthy internal model for acting appropriately. This is lacking due to one or more of the following; neglect, abuse, abrupt separation, frequent interruption of or lack of responsiveness in the primary care giver.

Without treatment they are likely to end up as sociopaths (lacking the ability to relate to others, devoid of social conscience and unable to trust others.

Cycle of privation

It has been suggested that privation (and to a lesser extent deprivation) can lead to a cycle of privation: as the child becomes an adult and has children of their own, they are driven to create the same deprived conditions for their children as they endured. People who have suffered privation as a child may find it difficult to start and maintain relationships and often do not have partners to help with child-rearing.

Are the effects reversible?

There has been research showing that the effects of disruption are reversible.

A study by Triseliotis (1984) looked at 44 adults who had been adopted as children. They were suffering the effects of disruption when they were taken for adoption and were not expected to recover, but with good care they did recover and were later classed as well-adjusted.

Curtiss's study of Genie (1977) showed the effects of privation were extensive and permanent, but the care she received once found was sporadic and inconsistent. She was 13 when found, and so the window of opportunity for development (critical period) had passed.

Koluchová (1976, 1991) studied twin Czech boys, found at 7 years old, suffering the effects of privation (delayed cognitive, emotional, social and physical development). The boys had very good care after they were found, being adopted by sisters into secure families. With that care, the Czech twins were able to live normal lives. Both boys caught up in school, got jobs and built healthy productive relationships resulting in a full recovery. It is debatable however, whether the twins were deprived rather than subject to privation: they had formed an attachment to each other prior to their ill treatment. They were also found within their critical period of development.

Case study: Attachment and Trauma network

Research on disruption to attachment is used by many organisations that try to help children and adults. One example is the Attachment and Trauma Network (www.attachmenttraumanetwork.com/education.html), which provides guidance, support and education for carers of traumatised children. The research forms the basis for how to treat such children in the most efficient manner, depending on the experiences they have had.

References

BOWLBY, J. (1944) Forty-Four Juvenile Thieves: Their Characters and Their Home Life. *International Journal of Psychoanalysis*. 25. pp.107–27.

CHARLES, H. Z. & GLEASON, M. M. (2010) Reactive Attachment Disorder: A Review for DSM V, *American Psychiatric Association*.

CURTISS, S. (1977) *Genie: A psycholinguistic Study of a Modern-Day 'Wild Child'*. London: Academic Press.

HODGES, J. & TIZARD, B. (1989) Social and Family Relationships of Ex-institutional Adolescents. *Journal of Child Psychology and Psychiatry*. 30. pp.77–97.

KOLUCHOVÁ, J. (1976) The Further Development of Twins after Severe and Prolonged Deprivation: A Second Report. *Journal of Child Psychology and Psychiatry*. 17. pp.181–8.

KOLUCHOVÁ, J. (1991) Severely Deprived Twins after Twenty-Two Years' Observation. *Studia Psychologica*. 33. pp.23–8.

QUINTON, D. et al (1985) Institutional Rearing, Parenting Difficulties and Marital Support. *Annual Progress in Child Psychiatry and Child Development*. pp.173–206.

ROBERTSON, J. & ROBERTSON, J. (1969) *Young Children in Brief Separation Film Series*. Film Series, Concord Video and Film Council. New York: University of Film Library.

TRISELIOTIS, J. (1984) Identity and Security in Adoption and Long-Term Fostering. *Early Child Development and Care* 15 (2–3). pp.149–70.

Attachment: types

In psychology 'attachment' describes a strong emotional and reciprocal bond between two people, especially between an infant and its main caregiver(s). Attachment can be categorised into different types, depending on the quality of the bond. The quality of attachment is thought to influence all future relationships.

Research: Ainsworth & Bell's 'Strange situation' study

Ainsworth & Bell (1970) decided to investigate whether there were different types of attachment and what behaviour the different types produced. They created a controlled observation, called the 'Strange situation' study. The aim of the study was to see how children aged 12 to 18 months and their mothers acted and reacted in an unfamiliar situation (hence the study's name). It included mother and child being parted, the child being left with a stranger, and the child being left alone.

See also:
Attachments:
disruption and
privation.

The procedure was to guide the mother and child to a room specially treated to resemble a playroom, with toys and furniture in it. The pair were left alone for a short while and were observed unobtrusively and also recorded on film.

There were episodes of eight separations and reunions which activated attachment behaviour.

The sequence of separations and departures in the strange situation:

1	Mother and infant come into the room. There are two chairs to one side of the room and toys on the floor for the child to play with. Mother sits on a chair and reads a magazine; the child is left on the floor to explore the toys.
2	After 3 minutes the researcher enters the room and sits on the other chair in the room, briefly talking to the mother.
3	The stranger then goes to the child and attempts to communicate and play with the child.
4	The mother departs the room, leaving the stranger behind. The stranger offers comfort to the child if necessary and plays with the child.
5	The mother returns after 3 minutes and the stranger leaves the room.
6	After 3 minutes the mother leaves the room, leaving the child alone for a short while.
7	The stranger re-enters the room and gives comfort if needed and will also play with the child.
8	The mother returns to the room and the stranger leaves.

Each episode was designed to observe specific behaviour:

(1) episode 1–2 how effectively does the child use the mother as a secure base

(2) episode 3–4 If the child displays stranger anxiety (fear)

(3) episode 5 reunion behaviour

(4) episode 6–7 separation anxiety

(5) episode 8 reunion behaviour

There were a group of observers recording the child's behaviour every 15 seconds. Each of the behaviours being observed from the episodes was rated between 1–7 on degree of intensity of: (1) proximity and contact-seeking behaviour; (2) contact-maintaining behaviour; (3) proximity and level of avoidance/interaction with the stranger; (4) contact and/ or resisting behaviour; and (5) seeking behaviour.

A scoring system was used to record the reunion behaviour of the mother and child after each separation, as well the child's willingness to explore the environment, mother/child interaction, and stranger anxiety (how the child reacted to the stranger).

Types of attachment

From the results of the study, three types of attachment were identified:

➤ **securely attached** – These children were quite upset by the mother's departure, but were easily calmed and were enthusiastic on her return. This type of child was happy to explore the environment and interact with the stranger when the mother is present (66% of the children fell into this category)

➤ **insecure: anxious/avoidant** – These children were not that bothered about the mother's departure and did not really make an effort to re-acquaint themselves on her return; the children would actually turn away from the mother to avoid contact with her (22%)

➤ **insecure: anxious/resistant** – These children clung to the mother and protested at her departure, and in some cases were distraught on her departure and inconsolable. On the return of the mother, the children were at once clingy and distant, wanting to be held but pulling away from the affection once given (12%).

It was suggested that mothers' sensitivity had a large impact on the type of attachment displayed by the children. Mothers who were empathetic to their children's needs and responded aptly were more likely to have secure children than the mothers who lacked sensitivity to their children's needs.

Cross-cultural variation

Van Ijzendoorn & Kroonenberg (1988) carried out a meta-analysis of 32 studies across eight countries and found differences in attachment type between different countries. However, they found the prevailing type of attachment in all countries is that of 'securely attached'.

They also found that:

➤ Insecure-avoidant was the second most common in five out of the eight countries.

➤ In West Germany there was a very high rate of insecure-avoidant types compared to the other countries.

➤ In Japan and Israel, insecure–resistant was the second most common type, with very low levels of insecure-avoidant.

➤ The study also showed China had an equal split between insecure-avoidant and insecure-resistant children.

The researchers concluded that the varying parenting styles in different cultures did have an impact on the types of attachment displayed.

Benefits of the 'Strange situation' study
This study provided a way of gathering data on attachment in a quick, efficient and replicable manner. It triggered a vast increase in research in the area of attachment and allowed this area to progress rapidly. The study has been repeated many times, internationally.

Criticisms of the 'Strange situation' study

➤ Ecological validity – The experiment was criticised for lacking ecological validity as it was carried out in a laboratory setting, but Ainsworth argued that the situation was similar to many children's experience, e.g. when being left at a childminder or a playgroup.

➤ There is also the possibility that the mother may not have been the child's main caregiver, therefore the reactions may not have been a true indication of the child's attachment type in general, but rather just to a secondary carer.

See also:
Research:
reliability &
validity.

➤ Participant effects – It is possible that the mother's behaviour was affected by the environment, so interactions that were recorded and assumptions made about the mother's part in the relationship could have been affected by this.

➤ Ethical issues – The children were purposely put into a stressful situation, which could have had a psychological effect on them.

➤ Cultural bias – The study was possibly culturally biased, having been developed in the USA.

Temperament hypothesis

In 1984 Kagan presented his temperament hypothesis and has defined two types; inhibited (shy, timid, fearful) and uninhibited (bold, sociable and gregarious behaviour). His theory is that the inhibited babies will be less likely to form attachments and so achieve secure attachment easily, compared to the unhibited babies. In 2008 Moehler included Kagan in a study to see if adult relationships were affected by infant behaviour characteristics, using crying and motor skills as the measure of infant behaviour. He found these characteristics did indeed have an impact of future relationship skills dependent on environment interaction. Kagan suggests that genes and environment are highly influential in this process

Several studies have supported this theory, such as Belsky & Rovine (1987) who studied babies in their first few days of life and then later looked at their attachment types and found babies who had been happy content babies had more likelihood of a secure attachment than babies who were very anxious and difficult to get to sleep and feed.

In relation to disruption and privation, it is likely that children who are naturally of a calmer disposition will have more possibility in overcoming a bad start as they will be more receptive to help.

In relation to formation of attachment the babies who are easier to spend time with are more likely to have their needs met by their mother in the amount of attention they receive and so more likely to form a healthy monotropic bond.

The influence of attachment on adult relationships

Hazen & Shaver (1987) noticed that romantic couples have many of the relationship characteristics of children to caregiver, such as a dependency on each other and wanting to spend as much time as possible with each other. They decided to test the observation and see if the quality of childhood attachment had any impact on their adult relationship styles. They published a love quiz in an American newspaper and collected data from people about their early attachments, and information about their current romantic relationships. Results showed that:

➤ Adults who had a secure attachment in early childhood were more likely to have fulfilling loving relationships; they felt love was enduring and based on mutual trust.

➤ People who had early insecure attachments were more cynical about love and more likely to have been through divorce or separation; they felt love was a rare thing.

Application
There are many programmes that use the findings and theories of Ainsworth and Bowlby, such as the ABC programme, used in the New Orleans Intervention Tulane team in helping children who have been mistreated and then fostered.

References

AINSWORTH, M. D. S. & Bell, S. M. (1970) Attachment, Exploration, and Separation: Illustrated by the Behavior of One-Year-Olds in a Strange Situation. *Child Development*. 41. pp.49–65.

BELSKY, J. & ROVINE, M. (1987) Temperament and Attachment Security in the Strange Situation: An Empirical Rapprochement. *Child Development*. 58. pp.787–95.

HAZAN, C. & SHAVER, P. R. (1987) Romantic Love Conceptualised as an Attachment Process. *Journal of Personality and Social Psychology.* 52. pp.511–24.

MOEHLER, E. et al (March 2008). Infant Predictors of Behavioral Inhibition. *British Journal of Developmental Psychology* 26 (1). pp.145–50.

VAN IJZENDOORN, M. H. & KROONENBERG, P. M. (1988) Cross-Cultural Patterns of Attachment: A Meta-analysis of the Strange Situation. *Child Development*. 59. pp.147–56.

Biological rhythms

Biological rhythms are regular changes in biological activity. There are three types: ultradian, circadian and infradian. The rhythms are controlled by mechanisms in the brain called endogenous pacemakers (EPs). Biological rhythms can be influenced by external factors such as daylight. These influences are called exogenous zeitgebers (EZs).

Role of EPs and EZs

Endogenous pacemakers (EPs) are thought to be genetic mechanisms that create the biological rhythms of the body. Even unborn babies have a pattern of activity and rest in the womb, which offers evidence for the existence and the importance of endogenous pacemakers. The exogenous zeitgebers (EZs) help the body synchronise to the rhythms of the outside world. The main one is light, but social cues can also be significant. This rhythm synchronisation is vital among animals as it is a key to survival, for example telling the animal when it is night or day and so whether to hide from predators or forage for food.

The pineal gland is the main EP in birds and some mammals. It works through a process of light (EZ) triggering activity in nerve cells. Serotonin then converts to melatonin, which is released into the circulation and has an effect on the rhythmic activity of the body via organs and glands.

The main EP in most mammals, and humans, is the suprachiasmatic nucleus (SCN), which follows a more complex pathway than the pineal gland. It is a small cluster of cells in the hypothalamus which regulate the creation and secretion of melatonin in the pineal gland. Another pathway connects the SCN to the retina. Light then activates the SCN nerve cells and causes an indirect release of melatonin. The SCN and pineal gland are here working as joint endogenous pacemakers.

Ultradian rhythm

These rhythms cover a period of fewer than 24 hours. They include the sleep cycle and digestive cycle. They also have several cycles in a 24-hour period, for example the sleep cycle fluctuates between lighter and deeper sleep several times throughout the sleep/wake cycle.

The sleep cycle is around 90 minutes for adults and 60 minutes for children and involves five stages of sleep. These are slow wave sleep (SWS) 1–4, and rapid eye movement (REM) sleep. SWS is often referred to as NREM (non-rapid eye movement).

➤ NREM stages 1 & 2 – relaxed state, easily woken, heart rate slows, temperature drops

➤ NREM stages 3 & 4 – metabolic rate (rate at which the body uses energy) slowest, growth hormone produced

➤ REM paradoxical – brain and eyes active, but body paralysed. The brain is at its most active.

There are several sleep cycles during a full night's sleep, and as the night goes on REM increases. You only enter NREM stages 1–2 at the beginning and end of all the sleep cycles.

Study

In 1967 Friedman & Fisher carried out a study on the digestive cycle. They observed psychiatric patients over a six-hour period and found a clear 90-minute cycle in their digestive habits. Their findings led to the conclusion that the human has a basic rest activity cycle (BRAC) which drives various habits and tells us when we need to eat.

This BRAC idea even links in with habits that have been acquired, such as smoking.

Circadian rhythm

These rhythms are around 24 hours and include the sleep/wake cycle and the temperature cycle. The sleep/wake cycle works in unison with the other rhythms, e.g. the ultradian cycle of sleep.

When there is no daylight the pineal gland releases the hormone melatonin, which causes drowsiness and so induces sleep. When light is present the pineal gland stops releasing melatonin so readily. This is why it is easier to stay awake when you are tired in the day, than at night. Daylight is the main EZ but there are others, like time prompts from clocks, and social cues like eating schedules.

Studies into the sleep cycle usually consist of depriving people of EZs, therefore putting them into 'temporal isolation'. This might involve removing their sense of time (awareness of day and night) or removing social cues such as eating patterns and noise (there is always more noise in the day than the night). These studies aim to find the natural rhythm of the body, our 'free running clock'. They are also interested in how far EZs influence our natural EPs, an influence known as 'entrainment'.

Study

In a study by Folkard et al (1985), participants lived in an isolated environment and had artificial cues as to when to get up in the morning (alarm clock set at 7.45am and lights came on) and when to go to sleep (clocks set at 11.45pm and lights went out). The researchers remotely changed the clocks, setting them either faster or slower, so effectively lengthening or shortening the days. The results showed that participants could tolerate the days being lengthened up to 28 hours, but were unable to tolerate days shorter than 22 hours.

This shows that the EPs will self-regulate when needed and will only be influenced by EZs to a degree.

Infradian rhythm

These rhythms are longer than a day, but no longer than a year. They include the menstrual cycle and seasonal affective disorder (SAD).

The human menstrual cycle is around every 28 days and is regulated by a group of hormones, including the follicle stimulating hormones (FSH), luteinizing hormone (LH), progesterone and oestrogen. In other mammals the menstrual cycle can be shorter or longer.

SAD is thought to be an effect of the lack of daylight during winter months, which leads to increased secretion of melatonin by the pineal gland. This may then lead to decreased levels of serotonin. Very low levels of serotonin are indicated as one of the contributors of depression.

Study
In 1967, Alain Reinberg reported the case of a woman who stayed in a cave for three months, away from EZs such as daylight and social cues. She found not only that her sleep/wake cycle increased a little (circadian rhythms), but also that her menstrual cycle decreased. After she left the cave, it took a year before her menstrual cycle was back to normal. This indicates that a lack of the major EZ light has far-reaching effects, i.e. it meant the circadian rhythm was not synchronised, which in turn disrupted other biological rhythms, such as the infradian rhythm. This shows the importance of maintaining biological rhythms and how it affects our physiology.

Other studies have shown that menstrual cycles can be affected by the presence of other women. Russell et al (1980) found that menstrual cycles synchronise. Another study (McClintock, 1971) showed that the menstrual cycle is also affected by the constant presence of men.

Case study: shift work and jet lag

Shift work and jet lag involve disruption to both the circadian and the ultradian rhythms. Shift workers are often working when they should be sleeping and the body has no chance to adjust the circadian rhythm, as the patterns of work (and sleep) are constantly changing. The ultradian rhythm is then often affected, as the quality of the sleep may be impaired. Research suggests that people who do shift work on a regular basis are likely to have their lifespan reduced by up to 10 years.

References

FOLKARD, S. et al (1985) Independence of the Circadian Rhythm in Alertness from the Sleep/Wake Cycle. *Nature*. 313. pp.678–9.

FRIEDMAN, S. & FISHER, C. (1967) On the Presence of a Rhythmic, Diurnal, Oral Instinctual Drive Cycle in Man: A Preliminary Report. *Journal of the American Psychoanalytic Association*. 15. pp.317–43.

McCLINTOCK, MARTHA, K. (January 1971). Menstrual Synchrony and Suppression. *Nature*. 229. pp.244–5.

REINBERG, A. (1967) Eclairment et cycle menstrual de la femme. *Rapport au Coloque International du CRNS. La photoregulation de la reproduction chez les oiseaux et les mammiferes*. Montpelier.

RUSSELL, M. J. et al (1980) Olfactory Influences on the Human Menstrual Cycle. *Pharmacology, Biochemistry and Behaviour*. 13. pp.737–8.

Conditioning: classical

Classical conditioning is a form of learnt behaviour, acquired via a process of association as a result of stimulus–response interaction. This type of conditioning is passive and, unlike operant conditioning, does not include a new behavioural response. As with much of behaviourism, research into classical conditioning was first carried out with animals, examining the conditioning of natural reflexes in response to a given stimulus.

Pavlov's dogs

The earliest research into classical conditioning was carried out by Pavlov (1927). Pavlov, a physiologist, was actually studying digestion in dogs and had developed a technique of collecting their saliva. He noticed the dogs tended to salivate in anticipation before their food was presented. He decided to test whether he could make the dogs salivate to a stimulus that was totally unrelated to the food.

The dog was confined to a space with strapping from a frame. The food was placed in front of the dog, which could be observed from the screen. When the food was introduced, the bell would ring. Finally, the dog would salivate without the presence of the food.

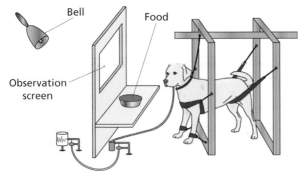

The following diagram shows how the conditioning happens. The first process is what happens naturally, i.e. an unconditioned response (UCR), salivation, occurs. In the second process, the bell (a neutral stimulus, NS)

is introduced with the food and still causes a natural response (UCR) to the food. The third process is where the NS has been introduced enough times with the food for the dog to salivate to the bell on its own. This means the stimulus and response are now conditioned.

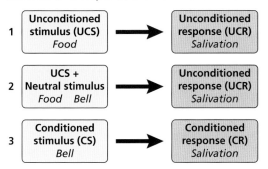

Types of classical conditioning

There are different types of classical conditioning, based on the timing of the NS with the UCS. They are outlined in the table, using the Pavlov dogs as an example.

Type	Procedure	Level of success
Delayed or forward	NS (bell) is presented before the UCS (food) and remains on whilst the UCS (food) is presented and until the UCR (salivation) appears.	The conditioning has been successful when the CS (bell) causes CR (salivation) without the UCS (food). An interval of half a second seems to produce the strongest learning. As the interval increases, the learning decreases.
Backward	The NS (bell) is presented after the UCS (food).	This type is generally not successful with lab animals, but advertising uses it to great success e.g. camera pans across a deserted beach with a hammock between palm trees; then the advert mentions a luxury holiday in Bali.
Simultaneous	The NS (bell) and the UCS (food) are presented together.	Conditioning has successfully happened when the CS (bell) produces the CR (salivation) without the UCS (food).

Type	Procedure	Level of success
Trace	The NS (bell) is presented and removed before the UCS (food) is presented. This leaves a 'memory trace' of the NS (bell) to cause conditioning.	The CR (salivation) is usually not as strong as in the delayed or simultaneous types.

Conditioning will last as long as the UCS (food) is offered from time to time with the CS (bell). The presentation of the UCS (food) periodically will reinforce the behaviour.

Other features of classical conditioning

Generalisation
This is where the CR transfers spontaneously to a stimulus similar to the CS. For example, if a certain pitch of bell was used for conditioning the dog to salivate and another sound of a similar pitch was then introduced, the dog would still salivate. It has generalised the bell sound. Yet, if the pitch becomes too different from the original CS (bell), the CR (salivation) will weaken and eventually cease. If the salivation stops, the dog is showing discrimination.

Extinction
This can happen if the CS is never reinforced by the presence of the UCS. The response will simply fade away.

Spontaneous recovery
This is what happens after a response has been extinguished. If the CS (bell) is presented again a few hours or days later, the conditioned response will probably reappear. For this reason, the elimination of a conditioned response usually requires more than one extinction session.

Higher-order conditioning
Suppose a dog has learnt to salivate to a bell. Now you present a flash of light before ringing the bell. If you repeat this several times, then the dog will eventually

salivate to the light (although it probably won't salivate as much as it did to the bell). This association of a new neutral stimulus with a previously conditioned stimulus is specifically called higher-order conditioning.

Research: Little Albert (Watson & Raynor)

Watson & Raynor (1920) were carrying out tests on a reportedly stable and unemotional child called Albert who was studied from 8 months to just over a year old. From prior tests, they had found the only thing that could upset Albert were severe sudden noises. They wanted to see if they could provoke a learned emotional response in Albert. They presented him with a variety of creatures, including a white rat, to which he showed no fear. Later they would present the rat to Albert again and, as he put his hand on the creature, they would hit a metal bar immediately behind his head, causing a fear reaction. After this happened several times, Albert was presented with the rat without the noise, causing him to react with intense fear to a stimuli not previously feared. They concluded behaviour was conditioned from the environment and experience. In little Albert's case he had become conditioned to fear rats, which in turn could have created a phobia (irrational fear).

Aversion and phobias

Although much of the initial research was carried out with non-humans, classical conditioning applies equally to humans and has multiple applications, such as; phobias connected to education (Boulton et al, 2001) and conditioned taste aversion (Capaldi, 1996).

An example of taste aversion is when a child refuses to eat vegetables, so the parent mixes them up with something the child likes, such as mashed potato. After the child has associated greens with a feeling of positive emotion toward a favoured food, they will be more willing to eat the greens on their own, resulting in a positive conditioned emotional response.

Phobias connected with education may span from a learnt fear of a neutral stimulus, such as a classroom, teacher or exams. This phobia generally happens without intention and can start from something small, such as an embarrassing event on a child's first day at school, to being publicly humiliated when a bad mark is read out in class. This might then cause the child to avoid school or not take an active part in lessons.

Case study: conditioned response

When Clare was around 6 years old, she ate a sprout that had a bug in it, which made her sick. Since then, Clare has felt ill at the sight of sprouts, or the smell of them cooking. She had formed an association that sprouts equal bugs, which in turn cause sickness. Classical conditioning links eating habits and eating disorders to an episode where there was pain or discomfort from eating (anorexia nervosa) or where food is associated with comfort (obesity).

References

BOUTON, M. E., et al (2001). A Modern Learning Theory Perspective on the Etiology of Panic Disorder. *Psychological Review. 108.* pp.4–32.

CAPALDI, E. D. (Ed.). (1996). *Why We Eat What We Eat: The Psychology of Eating.* Washington, D.C.: American Psychological Association.

PAVLOV, I. P. (1927). *Conditioned Reflexes: An Investigation of the Physiological Activity of the Cerebral Cortex* (translated by G.V. Anrep). London: Oxford University Press.

WATSON, J. B. & RAYNER, R. (1920) Conditioned Emotional Reactions. *Journal of Experimental Psychology. 3(1).* pp.1–14.

Conditioning: operant

Operant conditioning is an explanation of learning developed by behavioural psychologist B.F. Skinner (1938). According to this theory, positive and negative reinforcement will strengthen desired behaviour whereas punishment will weaken undesirable behaviour.

Thorndike's puzzle box

Thorndike (1911) was interested in how new behaviours were learnt. He observed how a kitten learned to escape from a 'puzzle box' by pressing a lever, something it first did by accident (trial and error). It gradually became quicker and quicker at escaping. Thorndike concluded that successful behaviour led to the behaviour being repeated in similar circumstances – his 'law of effect' theory.

Skinner's research

Skinner built on Thorndike's work, maximising the objectivity of his observations by creating a chamber where rats or pigeons could be monitored and controlled – the 'Skinner box'. Like kittens, the rats and pigeons would mostly do irrelevant actions, but by accident might hit a mechanism that released a food pellet. They learned to increase the frequency of the accidental behaviour to get the food. Skinner used the term 'operant conditioning' to describe this type of learning where behaviour is influenced by the consequences that follow it.

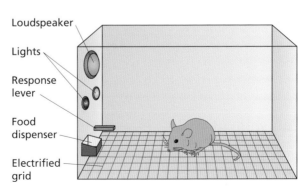

Loudspeaker
Lights
Response lever
Food dispenser
Electrified grid

Reinforcement

Operant conditioning depends on reinforcement (reward), the process by which a behaviour is strengthened. Reinforcement may be positive or negative:

➤ **Positive reinforcement** is a reward given after a desired behaviour occurs. This reward encourages the behaviour to be repeated.

➤ **Negative reinforcement** is where a creature performs a behaviour in order to avoid something unpleasant, e.g. the rat needs to press a lever to stop an electric shock. This is still a reward, but instead of receiving something pleasant for a desired behaviour, something unpleasant is avoided by performing the behaviour.

Reinforcers may also be categorised as primary (when the reward meets a basic biological need, such as food) or secondary (e.g. money, which doesn't meet a basic need itself but gives you the power to do so).

Case study: reinforcement

A mother and child are in a supermarket. The child screams for sweets and the mother gives them. The child has just been positively reinforced for the screaming. The child will continue with the behaviour every time he is in the supermarket. The mother has been negatively reinforced, because her action of  giving the sweet avoids the unpleasantness of the screaming in public. She will continue to give the child sweets in the supermarket.

Punishment

Unlike positive and negative reinforcement, punishment has no pleasant effects. It is meant to weaken behaviour. For example, a young child is put on the naughty step every time he behaves badly. The child does not like being on the naughty step, so learns to stop behaving badly.

Note that both positive and negative reinforcement make a behaviour more likely, whereas punishment makes a behaviour less likely.

Types of reinforcement

Skinner went on to identify different reinforcement types:

➤ Continuous reinforcement involves getting a reward every time a behaviour is performed. However, if reward is withheld, the behaviour will quickly disappear.

➤ In a fixed ratio schedule (FR), reward is related to the number of behaviours performed, e.g. factory workers being paid for every batch of 150 items. This schedule produces high steady response rates but if the reward is not given, the behaviour will disappear rapidly.

➤ Variable ratio schedules only reward after several responses, and the level of reward will vary. Like FR, response rates are high. This pattern of reinforcement achieves the fastest response rate and is less likely to disappear when reward is not given. Gambling systems work on this idea, e.g. people play the lottery week after week, and may only win small amounts now and then, but keep on gambling in the hope of the big reward.

➤ Fixed interval schedule, provides regular reinforcement but may result in an uneven patterns of response. For example, if a child gets pocket money every Saturday for keeping her room clean, she may forget about the chore until Friday night, where there will be a rush of activity to get the reward on Saturday. This has a rapid disappearance if the reward is withheld, and behaviour tends to be sporadic.

Evaluation of operant conditioning

Strengths

➤ Operant conditioning provides a convincing explanation of the way in which we learn and maintain types of behaviour, e.g. language and phobias.

➤ Operant conditioning enables humans and animals to behave efficiently as they learn to perform behaviours that have most success, e.g. in finding food or mates.

➤ Much of the research has been carried out in controlled conditions in laboratories, so findings can be replicated.

Weaknesses

➤ Instinctive drift – Breland and Breland 1951 found that animals that have been taught behaviours via operant conditioning tend to 'drift back' towards instinctive behaviours, especially if the learned behaviour was an unnatural one (e.g. a rat pressing a lever), proving the effect of the condtioning is not lasting.

➤ Most experiments on operant conditioning use animals, raising ethical issues. Also, they tend to be laboratory experiments, raising questions about ecological validity.

➤ Some critics have argued that classical conditioning is actually responsible for much of the behaviour that researchers have described as operant conditioning.

See also:
Conditioning:
classical.

References

BRELAND, K. & BRELAND, M. (1951) A Field of Applied Animal Psychology. *American Psychologist*. 6. pp.202–4.

SKINNER, B. F. (1938) *The Behaviour of Organisms*. New York: Appleton-Century-Crofts.

Thorndike, E. L. (1911) *Animal Intelligence: Experimental Studies*. New York: Macmillan.

Conformity

This is an aspect of social psychology. It looks at why people follow the behaviour of others (conform), due to real or imagined pressure. There are several types of conformity, the two main ones being majority influence (where people follow the masses) and minority influence (where people follow the minority).

Majority influence

Types of majority influence

For many years the dominant theory of majority influence has been that of Deutsch & Gerard (1955), who identified two types of majority influence:

	Normative influence	Informational influence
Motivation	The person wants to fit in with others and be liked/accepted.	A person who is unsure of what is going on, or is self-conscious, will follow others who they think know what they are doing. The person wants to be correct.
Process	The person conforms publicly but not privately. The person may not agree with the majority, but pretend to do so in public.	The person will conform publicly and privately, believing that others know something the person doesn't.
Example	A person starts a new job and pretends to be amused by the jokes of colleagues. The person wants to be accepted and liked.	A person starts a new job and follows how others do the same job, believing it to be correct.

Conformity in ambiguous situations

In 1935, Sherif investigated whether people would think independently in an uncertain situation, or would conform to the judgement of others. His study used an optical illusion called the auto-kinetic effect, whereby a point of light in a dark room appears to move as the eyes attempt to focus on it. Sherif asked participants to focus on the light and to judge roughly how far the light moved (it doesn't actually move at all). Participants looked at the light in two conditions, on their own and in a small group, then estimated the movement.

Sherif found that, when in a group, participants would agree on one approximation of movement, but as individuals they had a variety of estimations. It was also found that after participants had been in a group, they always used the group estimate when asked alone, indicating that in a situation where there is no definite right or wrong answer people will accept the judgement of others as correct. This is an example of informational influence.

Conformity in non-ambiguous situations

Soloman Asch was interested in whether people would follow others, even if the answer was non-ambiguous (i.e. evident). In his 'line experiment' (1951), a participant had to match a standard line with three other lines shown. Asch also arranged for several confederates (people working with the researcher) to judge the line in a group along with the participant. The participant thought the confederates were participants. The genuine participant would be chosen to answer either last or last but one. The confederates had already been instructed to answer incorrectly in 12 out of 18 trials. Asch found around 74% of participants answered incorrectly with the group at least once and so were influenced by others in their judgement.

When later asked their judgement privately, most said they agreed with the group's incorrect answer because they didn't want to stand out. This exemplifies normative influence, as they changed their minds and answered correctly when alone. Other participants, though, believed the group knew something they didn't and privately still believed them to be correct – an example of informational influence.

Evaluating the research

The answers in the Asch study might be explained by the era in which it was conducted. The 1950s was a very conservative period in American history, with its anti-communist witch hunts. Accusations of being non-conformist would have alarmed many of the student participants.

Both studies could also be accused of lacking:

➤ ecological validity: not easily generalised beyond the context of the study)

➤ mundane realism (the task is not one that participants might do in real life).

Minority influence

Minority influence can be a very powerful force. It can lead to social change, with people undergoing a complete conversion to the minority view. Ironically, minority influence starts with a non-conformist, often referred to as a dissenter.

Factors important in minority influence

Moscovici (1969) suggests that minority influence is exerted due to behaviour style; in other words *what* the dissenter says is not as important as *how* it is said. According to Moscovici, the minority need to be 'forceful, persistent and unwavering, but at the same time, appear flexible and open-minded'.

Over time, the majority may forget who initiated the idea . This is call 'social crypto-amnesia'. One reason may be that the dissenter is not someone who is admired, and people don't want to acknowledge who they were influenced by.

Consistency

Consistency is seen as the most important factor. It needs to be present over time, both in the dissenter's viewpoint and between dissenters if there is more than one. (There is debate as to whether it is more influential to have a single dissenter or several.) Consistency is important because:

➤ It draws attention to the minority

➤ It gives an impression that the dissenter knows what they are talking about

➤ It sows the seeds of doubt in the majority.

Investment

Investment refers to how much the dissenter sacrifices for their viewpoint, such as risking having no friends or even giving up a more comfortable way of life. For example, during the Suffragette protests of the early 20th century, upper- and middle-class women swapped their comfortable existence for the hardship of prison, and a few ultimately gave their lives for the cause.

Autonomy
The dissenter must be seen to be acting out of principle and not for personal gratification.

Flexibility
The dissenter needs to be consistent, but not seen to be stubborn or dogmatic, which would alienate the majority. Rather than telling people what to think, they should show them how to think using persuasive argument.

Snowball effect

The term 'snowball effect' describes how the minority influences the majority slowly at first, but then increasingly, as more and more people start agreeing with the dissenter, publicly. Like a rolling snowball, support for the idea gains momentum as it becomes bigger. Eventually it gets so big that the minority view becomes the majority view, and social change has occurred. For example, 30 years ago only a few people were interested in recycling to save the planet, but through argument, investment of time and energy and initially a non-dogmatic approach, the idea has now become big business and, with the majority of people believing it too, has become majority influence.

Research: Consistency

A meta-analysis of 97 studies, carried out by Wood et al (1994), tested the consistency hypothesis and found it to be a major factor in minority influence.

One such study was by Moscovici et al (1969). Participants, who thought they were taking a colour perception task, were put into groups of six and had to identify the colour of 36 glass slides, all in varying shades of blue.

There were three groups:

➤ The consistent group had two confederates posing as participants; they were told to say every slide was green.

➤ The inconsistent group also had two confederates acting as the minority, but this time they were told to say the slides were green two out of three times.

➤ The control group had no confederates, so acted as a comparison for the previous two experimental groups.

Results showed that more than 8% of participants followed the minority in the consistent group, compared to 1.25% in the inconsistent group. When they were later given individual tests, participants who had been in the first two groups were more likely to say that an ambiguously-coloured slide (blue/green) was green, compared to those in the control group. These results support the consistency hypothesis, but also indicate that the minority have a longer-term influence.

Stengths

➤ Good experimental validity, as the studies were carried out in a controlled environment

➤ Reliability, as the studies were replicable and showed similar results when used again.

Weakness

➤ Poor ecological validity, as the environment was artificial and the results may only show how people react in a controlled environment, not in the real world.

Dual process theory

There is debate as to whether conformity is a single or a dual process. Single process means there is a continuum between majority and minority influence, so they are just opposite ends of the same process (Latane and Wolfe's 'Social Impact Theory' 1981). The dual process theory says that majority and minority influence are different in their process (Moscovici 1969):

Dual process theory The majority and minority exert influence differently	
Majority influence	**Minority influence**
Works quickly and is not as enduring as minority influence, as the majority don't need to think about their actions.	Is slower to take effect, as the majority have to go through a conversion before they will agree in public.
The minority are more likely to change only their public opinion, rather than their private views.	The majority will think about the minority view, internalise the thought, agree privately and then finally agree publicly.
The minority may also later conform privately.	According to Moscovici, dissenters encourage cognitive conflict, making the majority think analytically, and this process takes a while.
Even when they do agree publicly and privately, the conformity may be more temporary than in minority influence.	There will be more processing over a longer period.

References

ASCH, S. E. (1951) Effect of Group Pressure upon the Modification and Distortion of Judgements. In H. Guetzkow (Ed.) *Groups, Leadership and Men*. Pittsburgh, PA: Carnegie Press.

DEUTSCH, M. & GERARD, H. B. (1955) A Study of Normative and Informational Social Influence Upon Individual Judgements. *Journal of Abnormal & Social Psychology*. 51. pp.629–36.

LATANÉ, B. & WOLF, S. (1981) The Social Impact of Majorities and Minorities. *Psychological Review*. 88. pp.438–53.

MOSCOVICI, S. et al (1969) Influence of a Consistent Minority on the Responses of a Majority in Color Perception Task. *Sociometry*. 32. pp.365–80.

SHERIF, M. (1935) A Study of Social Factors Inperception. *Archives of Psychology*. 27. (Whole No. 187[c2]).

WOOD, W. et al (1994) Minority Influence: A Meta-analytic Review of Social Influence Processes. *Psychological Bulletin*. 115. pp.323–45.

Debates: free will & determinism

The debate here is whether humans are capable of self-determination (thinking for themselves; free will) or whether they are shaped or controlled by other factors. These factors may be external, such as experience of the world, or internal, such as genetic programming (determinism). The soft determinism view links both innate tendency and the availability of choice to act on those tendencies.

Free will

The approach most associated with free will is humanism. Maslow (1954) suggested that all humans have an innate drive to be autonomous (self-determined) in their efforts to meet self-actualisation. Carl Rogers (1959) suggested that people who do not take responsibility for themselves are unlikely to develop a good state of mental health.

See also:
Approaches:
humanist.

The importance of control in stress management supports these ideas. Marmot et al (1978) found that workers who felt they had no control over their work situation were more likely to develop a stress-related illness.

Determinism

The approaches most linked to determinism are biological, psychodynamic and behavioural.

See also:
Approaches:
biological.

The biological approach suggests we are either born with our behaviour or develop it due to a physical cause. Therefore we have no say in it. There is evidence both for and against the assumptions of this approach.

See also:
Approaches:
psychodynamic.

Behaviourism (learning theory) explains everything as a response to a stimulus, where there is no thought, just conditioned learning.

Social learning theory (Bandura, 1965) does take choice into account, however. For example, if a child observes an adult being aggressive to a doll and they see that

See also:
Approaches:
behavioural.

adult being punished, they are less likely to imitate the behaviour than if they had witnessed the adult being rewarded (or there being no consequences). This indicates some assessment of the situation prior to the behaviour. If that same child did imitate the behaviour, but was punished, they would also probably reconsider carrying out that behaviour again. A behaviourist would say this was evidence of operant conditioning (Skinner, 1938), with punishment weakening behaviour (determinism), but it is equally feasible that the child has reappraised the wisdom of the action and chosen not to do it (free will).

See also: Social learning theory.

Soft determinism

The cognitive approach is one of soft determinism: it brings together the ideas of free will and determinism and shows how they are integrated. Cognition is about how a person perceives a situation or task then assesses their capability of coping. If it is possible to change perception, it is also possible to think for oneself. In the same way, it is possible for the person to solve problems and respond selectively to a stimulus.

Soft determinism comes from the idea that a person is born with certain abilities and limitations, e.g. levels of intelligence are thought to be innate and set to a limit (therefore restricting how far they will develop academically).

Free will	Determinism
Strengths	
Society assumes people have a moral responsibility for themselves and others. Supporting free will would mean they are choosing to act properly or not.	Determinism is the basis of scientific investigation. If all acted on free will, predictions and patterns of behaviour could not exist.
People do make their own decisions and are therefore self-determining, showing free will.	Free will can be argued to be determined by brain activity, such as biochemical imbalance, which again supports the idea that behaviour is determined by our physiology and not a choice at all. This idea is supported by evidence that genetics do influence personality and behaviour (Walters & Whie, 1989).
Most people believe they have free will.	
Weaknesses	
Most theories on moral development agree that there are both internal and external forces involved. This would mean that moral development is a consequence of soft determinism, rather than of free will.	There is substantial evidence of genetic influence on behaviour, but it is highly improbable that genetics can be the full story, as concordance rates are never 100%. Even a genetic predisposition to a particular behaviour does not mean that a person will ever develop that behaviour. Force of will may be used to prevent it.
If people choose a particular path, that does not necessarily mean they have free will, as that path could have been pre-determined. There is also the problem of cultural relativism, as self-determination may only be appropriate behaviour in individualistic societies.	Even in the physical sciences, it is now widely accepted that nothing is 100% determined (Dennett, 2003). If nothing can be 100% predicted, there must be an element of free will or randomness.
If people class themselves as using free will, that is only a subjective judgement. It is not testable evidence that free will exists.	Determinists tend to over-simplify human behaviour and don't take into account the variables that could influence behaviour. Just because there is little evidence of free will, does not mean it doesn't exist and could be a vital factor in behaviour.

Case study: heredity and crime

In 1991, Stephen Mobley robbed a pizza store in California and shot John Collins, the manager, in the back of the head. He appealed his death sentence, arguing that he was 'born to kill'. Mobley had many aggressive criminal relatives. The appeal was rejected and Mobley was given a lethal injection in March 2005.

Walters & White's paper 'Heredity and Crime' (1989) presents a mass of evidence linking heredity to crime, which would support a determinist view. However, Mobley appeared to be proud of the fact he shot Collins, and also blamed Collins for making him do it, by crying. He seemed to take no responsibility for his own actions.

A cognitive soft deterministic view, might be that though he was genetically pre-disposed to be aggressive, he also the ability to control his aggression had he chosen to. A humanist might say it was his choice not to act self-responsibly, thus supporting a free will argument.

References

DENNET, D. C. (2003) http://ase.tufts.edu/cogstud/papers/SelfasaResponding.pdf

MARMOT, M. G. et al (1978) Employment Grade and Coronary Heart Disease in British Civil Servants. *Journal of Epidemiology and Community Health*. 32. pp.244–9.

MASLOW, A. (1954). *Motivation and Personality.* New York Harper Mobley v. State (1995) 265 Ga. 292

WALTERS, G. D. & White, T. W. (1989) Heredity and Crime: Bad Genes or Bad Research? *Criminology*. 27. p.3.

PETERSON, L. R. & PETERSON, M. J. (1959). Short-Term Retention of Individiual Verbal Items. *Journal of Experimental Psychology*. 58. pp.193–8.

SCHMOLCK, H. et al (2000) Memory Distortions Develop Over Time: Recollections of the O. J. Simpson Trial Verdict after 15 and 32 Months. *Psychological Science*. 11 (1). pp.39–45.

THOMSON, D.M. & TULVING, E. Associative Encoding and Retrieval: Weak and Strong Cues. *Journal of Experimental Psychology*. 86. pp.255–62.

TULVING, E. & PEARLSTONE, Z. (1966). Availability versus Accessibility of Information in Memory for Words. *Journal of Verbal Learning & Verbal Behavior.* 5 (4). pp.381–91.

TULVING, E. & PSOTKA, J. (1971) Retroactive Inhibition in Free Recall: Inaccessibility of Information Available in the Memory Store. *Journal of Experimental Psychology*. 87. pp.1–8.

UNDERWOOD, B. J. (1957) Interference and Forgetting. *Psychological Review*. 64. pp.49–60.

Debates: nature and nurture

The nature-nurture debate is one of the longest-running and most important in the field of psychology. The debate's central question focuses on the extent to which behaviour is caused by nature (genes) or nurture (environment). The reality seems to be a mixture of both on a continuum between the two extremes.

Nature: genes

The nativist view was exemplified by Plato and Descartes, both of whom believed a child starts life with knowledge and innate abilities already present at birth.

Darwin's evolutionary theory proposed that inheritance and adaptive behaviour were the key to survival. Psychologists took this further and argued that behaviour was the product of natural selection, within the environment of evolutionary adaptation (EEA), to secure reproductive success.

See also:
Approaches:
evolutionary.

The biological approach suggests that all behaviour is due to a physical cause of some sort, from one, or a combination, of genes, biochemical interaction, neuro-anatomical or through infection from micro-organisms.

See also:
Approaches:
biological.

To see behaviour as purely resulting from genetics is problematic, as there is substantial evidence that experience does alter development and behaviour. In studies looking at privation, Hodges and Tizard (1989) have shown that, given appropriate care, children's development and behaviour will be much improved. Their research also found that children brought up in a 'normal' environment had significantly better development and social skills than a comparable group, whose early privation impacted on their development and behaviour.

Nurture: environment

Nurturists, such as Watson (1913) and Skinner (1938), are firm in the idea that all behaviour is due only to experience. There is no question of innate ability, as we are all born with a blank slate (without knowledge or ability of any description). Interestingly, Locke, the man considered to have proposed the idea of the blank slate, did acknowledge the presence of innate ability.

Skinner suggested that behaviour was just a result of a series of stimulus-response interactions.

Skinner (1957) even proposed that language was purely a result of rewards and shaping, though this suggestion was challenged by Chomsky in the 1950s. Chomsky believed language was not only experienced through the environment, but through an innate ability for language in the brain. This idea is supported by the critical period in development, which suggests there is a window of opportunity, including for language. Once that stage has passed, the window is firmly closed.

In support of development via nurture, Martin et al found changes in the brain caused by the accumulation of experience. He found a change in biochemical balance in the brain after a series of psychotherapy sessions.

Interaction of genes and environment

There are three possible gene-environment interactions:

➤ **Passive**, where parental genes affect the way they treat their child. For example, if parents have a particular talent, such as being an artist, this may cause them to actively nurture artistic ability in the child.

➤ **Active**, where the child's genes cause the child to act in a particular way. For example, some children are more adventurous than others and will use their innate curiosity to interact with the world, therefore increasing IQ.

➤ **Reactive**, where a child has certain characteristics, such as a pleasing or displeasing temperament, or a particular striking feature. Parents and others in society may react to that characteristic, which in turn has an impact on development and behaviour.

The debate across different approaches

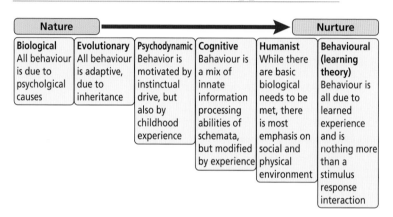

Nature					Nurture
Biological	**Evolutionary**	**Psychodynamic**	**Cognitive**	**Humanist**	**Behavioural**
All behaviour is due to psycholgical causes	All behaviour is adaptive, due to inheritance	Behavior is motivated by instinctual drive, but also by childhood experience	Bahaviour is a mix of innate information processing abilities of schemata, but modified by experience	While there are basic biological needs to be met, there is most emphasis on social and physical environment	**(learning theory)** Behaviour is all due to learned experience and is nothing more than a stimulus response interaction

Some controversial topics

Psychopathology (mental illness)

Both psychological and biological explanations have empirical evidence behind them. It is also clear that when a person suffering from a mental disorder is given a combination of biological and psychological treatment, such as drugs and psychotherapy, the treatment is much more effective than if only one method were used. It is now safer to say that it is better to look at a person holistically where both the biological (nature) and the effects of the environment (nurture) are taken into account. This holistic approach has become much more popular in recent years.

Intelligence

This debate is particularly important, with its implications for education policy and initiatives.

There is evidence to show that IQ is largely a result of genetics, though some research showing this does concede that nurture plays some part (Plomin et al, 1997).

There is also strong evidence to show that environment and experience play a large part, for example Eysenck & Evans (1994) found that IQ does not remain fixed, when they compared people at different educational stages. There is around a 10% difference in IQ between the undergraduate and general population, and others have shown that IQ tests are often culturally biased.

The importance of environment varies across different backgrounds. For instance, when a child from a deprived background takes part in stimulating educational activities, they will show more of a marked improvement in academic ability than a child engaged in the same activities from a wealthier background.

See also:
Approaches: behavioural;
Approaches: biological;
Approaches: evolutionary;
Issues: reductionism.

References

EYSENCK, H. & EVANS, D. (1994) Test Your IQ; What's Your Score? You Could Be a Genius! London: HarperCollins Publishers.

HODGES, J. & TIZARD, B. (1989) Social and Family Relationships of Ex-institutional Adolescents. *Journal of Child Psychology and Psychiatry.* 30. pp.77–97.

LOCKE. J. (1996) *An Essay Concerning Human Understanding,* Kenneth P. Winkler (ed.). 33–36. Indianapolis: Hackett Publishing Company.

PLOMIN, R. et al (1997) Nature, Nurture and Cognitive Development from 1-16 Years: A Parent-Offspring Adoption Study. *Psychological Science.* 8. pp.442–7.

SKINNER, B. F. (1938) *Science and Human Behaviour.* New York: Macmillan.

Disorders: depression

Depression is a mood disorder. It is a broad spectrum disorder that includes major depressive disorder (MDD) (also known as unipolar depression or clinical depression), as well as variations of depression, such as bipolar disorder (also known as manic depression).

Unipolar depression

Major depression affects about 10% of the population and is twice as likely to be diagnosed in women. In the case of peri-menopausal and menopausal women, it is five times more likely (Clayton & Ninan, 2010).

Symptoms and diagnosis

The symptoms are shown in the table. In order to be diagnosed with clinical depression, five or more symptoms have to be present continually for at least two weeks. Of these, two core symptoms must be present: (1) low or depressed mood, and (2) loss of interest or pleasure in daily activities.

There can be reliability and validity issues with diagnosis, especially as symptoms can vary greatly. There is also a possibility of gender bias because of the greater diagnosis in women, and of misdiagnosis due to cultural variation in presentation of symptoms.

Symptoms of unipolar depression

Social	Psychological
Not doing well in work or missing work	Continuous low mood or sadness
Seeking out fewer social events or activities than usual and avoiding social contact	Feelings of hopelessness and helplessness
Neglecting hobbies or interests that usually give pleasure	Low self-esteem
	Tearfulness
Difficulties in home life, due to own perspective and the expectations of others	Feeling guilt-ridden
Physical	Feeling irritable and intolerant to people who are usually liked
Moving and speaking more slowly than usual	Lack of motivation or interest in things that used to have the opposite effect
Change in appetite, either undereating or overeating	Difficulty in making decisions
Constipation	No enjoyment in things that used to give enjoyment
Unexplained aches and pains	
Lack of energy generally and often lack of interest in sex	Feelings of anxiety and worry
	Thoughts of self-harm or suicide
Changes of menstrual cycle, not caused by other factors, such as menopause	

Bipolar disorder

Bipolar disorder generally presents people in their twenties. Among sufferers, creative people seem to account for a higher than population average, including the writers Tennyson, Byron and Blake. In a survey by Jamison (1993) of 47 British distinguished writers and painters from the British Royal Academy, 38% had symptoms of bipolar disorder. Jamison suggested this finding gives evidence for the idea that the mania phase leads to a drive to create.

Symptoms of depression
On the depressive side, sufferers will have a number of the symptoms listed in MDD depression and for diagnosis will need to display low mood and/or lack of interest in everyday activities. The depression in bipolar disorder is

generally much more intense and severe than in MDD, leading to a high rate of suicide for those who have the energy to kill themselves. Dawson & Tylee (2000) called the depression 'lethargic melancholy'.

Symptoms of mania

Manic symptoms can be mild (hypomania) or extreme. A state of euphoria means sufferers could become delusional, with grandiose and unrealistic beliefs and ideas, e.g. believing they can run from Land's End to John O' Groats in a day (more than 1000 km). Other symptoms include: elevated and irritable mood, inflated self-esteem, a lack of inhibition, lack of sleep, racing thoughts and speech. The bouts of mania may be very brief or can go on for months. This phase can be exhausting and may lead to a brief time of peace in the mind of the sufferer, before they then plunge into the depression.

Diagnosis of bipolar depression

About 1% of people in the general population have a risk of developing bipolar disorder. Diagnostic criteria include having a distinct period of abnormal elevated mood, lasting at least a week, along with three other symptoms of mania and then a period of excessively low mood.

Biological explanations of depression

Genetic

The genetic explanation of depression suggests the disorder seems to run in families and the closer the family connection, the higher the likelihood of developing the disorder. Research also found that people who had a close relative with bi-polar depression were more likely to develop MDD than the general population and when the relationship was that of identical twins, there was a 3 times greater risk of the general population without relatives who had either disorder. (Gershon et al, 1989). Research by Hecimovic and Gilliam (2006) identified an abnormality in the 5-HHT gene with MDD sufferers, this gene is directly responsible for the levels of serotonin in the brain, a biochemical that is thought to be linked to MDD.

More recently, a UK led research team (Breen et al, 2011) found variations in chromosome 3p25-26. This finding was replicated by a US led research team, also looking at the genetic linkage with MDD (Pergadia et al, 2011). Replication of such findings is rare on two separate participant groups. Research is now under way in defining which genes are implicated from the 3p25-26 chromosome. As techniques of investigation have improved, it seems the aim of finding the definitive gene(s) responsible for MDD grows closer. This has huge implications for more effective treatment, as currently only around 50% of people are able to feel the full benefits of treatment on offer for MDD. Although many studies have supported the theory, if the cause were entirely genetic, then there would be 100% concordance rate (there never is). It is also difficult to separate environmental influences from biological. For example, twins will have very similar experiences, but may have identity issues that could impact on developing a depressive disorder.

See also:
Approaches:
biological.

Biochemical

Biochemical explanations look at the action of hormones and neurotransmitters. With MDD, the interaction of three particular neurotransmitters (serotonin, noradrenaline and dopamine) is of particular interest. The hormone cortisol, mostly associated with stress, is also implicated in depression, which could explain why people who are stressed become depressed. Support for the part these biochemicals play is shown in the effectiveness of drugs treating depression, e.g. SSRIs and MAOIs for MMD and lithium carbonate for bipolar sufferers. These drugs work by either helping or hindering the transmission of the biochemicals implied in each disorder.

Brain structure

The hippocampus has been found to be smaller in people with MDD than in the general population – though this might be due to stress, rather than being a cause of the disorder. Research is in its infancy in this area. A problem with brain structure as an explanation of psychopathology of any sort, is that it is not clear whether the structure caused the disorder, or the disorder caused the structure damage/difference.

Psychological explanations of depression

This covers theories from any approach other than biological, including:

Behavioural

Learned helplessness is one theory to explain reactive depression. Popularised by Seligman (1975), this suggests that through experience a person may come to feel helpless, believing they are unable to have any effect on their life. Seligman's theory was derived from putting dogs through inescapable and unavoidable stress in one condition and then finding that, when escape was possible, the dogs did not even try and get out. The dogs felt they couldn't win. Seligman generalised these findings to humans, suggesting that experiences and the situations people find themselves in can lead to them feeling inadequate and helpless.

Generalising from one species (dog) to another (human) is problematic, but Maier & Seligman (1976) did conduct a later study on humans and found the same result. There were contradictory findings though, showing that helplessness in one situation seemed to spur people on to succeed in later situations (Wortman & Brehm, 1975). It can also be criticised as not being a fully developed explanation, as it seems very limited both in explanation and in application, considering the variety of symptoms in depression.

Cognitive

Aaron Beck (1967) developed the 'cognitive triad' to explain depression, explaining that cognitive disortions and bias produced depression. Beck later added 'negative self-schemas', which are a set of beliefs and assumptions about oneself. He believed these 'negative self-schemas' are created out of previous traumatic experiences, such as the death of a parent. The problem with this idea is a lack of knowledge of how the person thought prior to their illness, and others have suggested that perhaps this negativity serves to keep the depression going, rather than causing it in the first place.

See also:
Approaches:
cognitive.

Diathesis-stress model

This is a combination of both biological and psychological factors. Diathesis is the biological and stress is the psychological. For example, a person may have a genetic predisposition (vulnerability) to MDD, but they will not develop the illness unless there is a trigger (stress) to set it off, such as a traumatic event (for example, the death of a relative). Brown & Harris (1989) did a retrospective study looking at people with depression and whether they had any major life event (trauma) occur just before presenting with the illness. They found there was a connection to major life events and underlying vulnerability.

Therapies

Biological (chemotherapy)

There are four main drug types for depression:

➤ MAOIs, which increase noradrenaline and serotonin

➤ tricyclics, which increase noradrenaline and serotonin

➤ SSRIs, such as Fluoxetine (Prozac) which are selective Serotonin re-uptake inhibitiors

➤ SNRIs, such as Venlafaxine which are selective noradrenaline re-uptake inhibitors.

SSRIs act similarly to TCAs, but are weak inhibitors for non-serotonin reabsorption and strong for serotonin and because of this there are fewer side effects. The SNRIs are strong on the inhibition of nor-adrenaline and serotonin and weaker on all others.

MAOIs have the worst recorded side-effects, including death. Tricyclics have fewer side-effects than MAOIs, and SSRIs don't have any obvious side effects (though the chance they might be implicated in people taking their own lives is increasing). There is such a variety of drugs available because there is no one drug that works for everyone. They are also not meant to be long term, which is a problem if no other treatment is given in conjunction with medication. Other problems include the time taken for the drugs to start working, as well as the possibility of dependency, tolerance and addiction.

See also: Therapies: biological.

If a person does not respond to any of the therapies offered, ECT (Electro-Convulsive Therapy) may be given.

Psychological therapy
Psychoanalysis tries to get at the reason for the depression, unlike the biological therapies that simply treat the symptoms. The aim is to release unresolved conflicts/ issues from the unconscious and then work through them, so the person can be freed from underlying emotions. The original version of psychoanalysis tended to take years without any real resolution, but briefer contemporary versions now take place, psychodynamic psychotherapy and Sullivan's interpersonal psychotherapy (IPT).

Case study: Diagnosing and treating depression

Carla has always been a cheerful and optimistic person, but this changed after her partner died of cancer a year ago. She has now lost her job, owing to her poor performance, negative attitude, lateness and absences since his death. She no longer answers the phone or the door. She used to enjoy an active social life but now just can't be bothered with anything or anyone.

Carla is suffering from MDD, as her symptoms have continued for more than two weeks and she has the two core symptoms of low mood and loss of pleasure in everyday activities. It seems to have started as a reaction to losing her partner (reactive depression), but has now become a chronic problem. She needs to have medication in the short term from her doctor, to lift her mood, so that she can be referred for therapy, possibly CBT.

References

AMERICAN PSYCHIATRIC ASSOCIATION (2013) *Diagnostic and Statistical Manual of Mental Disorders*. 5th Ed. Arlington, VA: American Psychiatric Publishing.

BREEN, G, et al (2011) A Genome-Wide Significant Linkage for Severe Depression on Chromosome 3: The Depression Network Study. *American Journal of Psychiatry. 168.* pp.840–7.

CLAYTON, A. H. & NINAN, P. T. (2010) Depression or Menopause? Presentation and Management of Major Depressive Disorder in Perimenopausal and Postmenopausal Women. *Primary Care Companion Journal of Clinical Psychiatry*. 12 (1).

DAWSON, A. & TYLEE, A. (eds.) (2000) Cited in (2001) *Depression: Social and Economic Timebomb*. London: BMJ Books.

JAMISON, K. R. (1993) *Touched with Fire: Manic-Depressive Illness and the Artistic Temperament*. New York: The Free Press.

McGUFFIN, P. et al (1996) A Hospital-based Twin Register of the Heritability of DSM-IV Unipolar Depression. *Arch Gen Psychiatry*. 53. pp.129–36.

PERGADIA, M. L. et al, A 3p26-3p25 Genetic Linkage Finding for DSM-IV Major Depression in Heavy Smoking Families. *American Journal of Psychiatry* (published online May 16, 2011; doi: 10.1176/appi.ajp.2011.10091319)

SELIGMAN, M. E. P. (1975) *Helplessness: On Depression, Development and Death*. London: W. H. Freeman.

Disorders: OCD

As the name suggests, obsessive-compulsive disorder (OCD) consists of obsessions and compulsions. The obsessions originate from something that a sufferer is afraid of and the compulsions are the actions they are driven to carry out, in order to ease that fear. OCD now has a classification of its own in the new DSM 5 (2013) and no longer comes under the general category of anxiety disorders.

Obsessions and compulsions

Obsessions are recurring, persistent thoughts, images or impulses that intrude on a person's life. They go beyond normal worries and anxieties and lead to repetitive and compulsive behaviour.

Compulsions are repetitive and ritualistic behaviours, such as repeated hand washing. The compulsions can also be psychological, such as carrying out a certain number of knocks on a door. The person feels they have no choice but to carry out the compulsions, being driven by the obsessions. This only increases their anxiety levels. In turn their obsessions intrude further, creating a vicious circle.

Symptoms of OCD

Obsessions include the following:

➤ Fear of contamination from germs, dirt or other people/ animals

➤ Fear of causing harm to self or others

➤ Unacceptable and unwanted thoughts that include violence, sex and/or aggression

➤ Scrupulosity: the need to do the right thing in order not to go against strongly-held views on religion and/ or morals

➤ Order and symmetry: the idea that everything must line up perfectly

➤ Superstitions: excessive attention to something considered lucky or unlucky.

Compulsions include the following:

➤ Constant checking and re-checking, for example that light switches are off

➤ Excessive monitoring of loved ones, such as texting them countless times a day to check they are safe

➤ Keeping everything in order, for example a carpenter having to arrange his tools in a particular way

➤ Excessive washing of hands and cleaning

➤ Rituals and excessive praying.

Diagnosis

In order to be classified with OCD, the sufferer needs to be assessed according to a scale of range and severity, such as the Yale-Brown Obsessive Compulsive Scale (DY-BOCS) (Rosario-Campos et al, 2006).

Depending on the country of residence, the person with such a disorder will be diagnosed from criteria present in a classification and diagnostic manual, for example the DSM 5 published by the American Psychiatric Association (APA). To be diagnosed, the obsessions and compulsions need to interfere with a person's life and take at least one hour a day every day. The compulsions would be those actions that are repetitive, inappropriate and out of proportion to the real or imagined threat. (APA 2013).

Most OCD sufferers will experience the symptoms for the majority of the time through the day.

Biological explanations

Genetic
Research has shown OCD sufferers often have family members on the OCD spectrum, implying a possible genetic link. The identified gene is sapap3 (Wan et al, 2012), but research so far is inconclusive.

Biochemical
Genes have also been linked to explanations concerning serotonin (hSERT gene) and glutamate (SLC1A1 gene). Both these genes help create transporters to mop up excess serotonin and glutamate after firing from one nerve cell to another. They can operate too quickly, before the messages have been sent.

Serotonin in particular would seem to be a significant factor in the development of OCD, but research is still at a very early stage and not enough is yet known to believe in this explanation completely.

Neuroanatomical
This explanation centres round the impulse circuit of the brain, in particular the orbito-frontal cortex (OFC). When the circuit is activated, the person feels compelled to act on the impulse, which normally causes the impulse to disappear. It is thought that, in an OCD sufferer, the brain does not switch off the impulse. Drugs are designed to modify the triggers. However, the drugs do not work on all sufferers, so it seems likely that there is another explanation.

Psychological explanations

Psychodynamic
According to these explanations, the disorder is a result of not being able to cope with unacceptable impulses and thought.

From a Freudian perspective, this could be seen as the inability to totally repress unacceptable wishes and impulses. This does seem credible, but psychoanalysis has been shown not to work in treating OCD and has even shown a worsening effect of the condition (Salzman, 1980).

According to Adler (1931), the disorder arises from the person having developed a feeling of inferiority during childhood and then acquiring compulsive ritualistic behaviour in order to overcome this feeling, by helping them gain control.

A problem with psychodynamic theories is the lack of evidential support in the public domain for effective treatment of OCD derived from this approach.

Behavioural

These explanations focus on conditioning. Obsessions arise from a process of classical conditioning; the anxieties arising from that cause the compulsive actions, which provide some relief and give positive reinforcement – so from the operant conditioning theory.

A weakness of behavioural explanations is that they do not explain the initiation of behaviour. However, therapies from this approach, such as exposure and response prevention therapy (ERP) have proved quite effective (Albucher et al, 1998), although this might be more to do with treating the maintenance of a compulsion, rather than its initial cause.

Cognitive

These explanations centre round the development of faulty thought patterns. Rachman (1997) found that OCD results from the suppression of catastrophic and intrusive thoughts. This is supported by by Salkovskis & Kirk's study (1997) which found that the more patients tried to suppress their intrusive thoughts, the more those thoughts grew.

A weakness of cognitive explanations is that they do not usually explain how the thoughts got there in the first place, though cognitive behavioural therapies have had some success in treating the disorder.

Case study: OCD

Suzanne is the mother of two young children and lives in fear that she will go to their room in the night and strangle them with their dressing robe cords. These thoughts intrude on her mind constantly (obsession). Due to her fear, she constantly feels anxious, which causes her psychological and even physical pain. Every night she has to go to their room and knot the cords repeatedly. This eases her discomfort for a short while, but then she will need to go to their room again and hide the cords. She does these actions repeatedly to alleviate her anxiety (compulsion).

References

ALBUCHER, R. C. et al (1998) Defense Mechanism Changes in Successfully Treating Patients with Obsessive-compulsive Disorder. *American Journal of Psychiatry*. 155 (4). pp.558–9.

ROSARIO-CAMPOS, M. C. et al (2006) The Dimensional Yale-Brown Obsessive-Compulsive Scale (DY-BOCS): An Instrument for Assessing Obsessive-Compulsive Symptom Dimensions. *Molecular Psychiatry*. 5. pp.495–504.

PIGOTT, T. A & SEAY, S. M. (1999) A Review of the Efficacy of Selective Serotonin Reuptake Inhibitors in Obsessive-Compulsive Disorder. *Journal of Clinical Psychiatry*. Vol 60 (2). pp.101–6.

RACHMAN, S. (1998) A Cognitive Theory of Obsessions: Elaborations. *Behaviour Research and Therapy*. 36. pp.385–410.

SALKOVSKIS, P. M. & KIRK, J. (1997) Obsessive Compulsive Disorder; In CLARK, D. M. & FAIRBURN, C. (eds.) *The Science and Practice of Cognitive Behavioural Therapy*. Oxford: Oxford University Press.

Disorders: phobias

All anxiety disorders involve an excessive psychological and physical fear reaction to a real or imagined stress. Phobias are irrational fears. The fear comes from a combination of factors which can be: cognitive (expectation of being harmed in some way); physical (fight or flight body response to a stressor); emotional (dread, terror and panic) or behavioural, such as running away or freezing up.

Types of phobia

Phobias may be:

➤ direct, or simple, such as arachnophobia (fear of spiders)

➤ indirect, or complex, such as claustrophobia (fear of closed-in spaces). The sufferer is not afraid of the space itself, but is afraid of the possible consequences of being trapped there. Therefore the danger feared is not directly from the situation but from the catastrophe the situation might cause.

The most common types of phobia are specific phobias, social phobia and agoraphobia.

Specific phobias
These are phobias where the person fears a specific thing that they feel will cause them harm directly. There are three sub-categories:

1. Animate objects, or fear of living creatures, such as spiders, frogs and mice

2. Inanimate objects or situations, such as fear of the dark, heights and needles

3. Illness, fear of death, disease and injury.

Social phobia (social anxiety disorder)
This complex phobia involves a person fearing judgement from others; a fear of embarrassment or humiliation in front of others. It is most common in adolescence.

Agoraphobia

This complex phobia involves a fear of open and public spaces where crowds gather. The sufferer fears something terrible will happen if they are exposed to a place beyond their comfort zone. It is most common in young women.

Cultural and gender variations

There seems to be cross-cultural variation in phobias. For example, in China 'Pa Leng' is fear of the cold. It is thought to derive from the philosophy of Yin/Yang, where cold and windy weather is believed to be energy sapping (McNally, 1997). If culture does have an impact, it must mean environment is at least partially responsible for phobias. There is also gender variation. For example, only 7 per cent of men but 16 per cent of women are fearful of water or heights (Kessler et al, 1994).

Diagnosis

According to the *Diagnostic and Statistical Manual of Mental Disorders5 (DSM 5)*, the phobic no longer has to recognise that their disorder is excessive to be diagnosed. Instead, the fear has to be out of proportion to the danger or threat, and symptoms of fear must be persistently present for at least six months. The sufferer will have a constant need to either avoid or escape the object or situation of fear, and the symptoms cannot be due to any other disorder. Social phobia and agoraphobia often intrude into daily functions of life, though with a specific phobia this is generally not the case.

Biological explanations of phobia

Biological explanations focus mainly on the autonomic nervous system (ANS) and genetics. The ANS directly relates to arousal levels. Lacey (1967) suggested that arousal reactions vary between people who have anxiety disorders, and those who do not. He described these differences as being on a continuum between stable and labile, with those who are labile being more easily aroused by a range of stimuli.

Some phobias seem to run in families, such as fear of blood and injections. Ost (1992) and Ayala (2009) found 64 per cent of people with such phobias had at least one first-degree family member with the same phobia. Evidence from twin studies into phobias by Kendler et al (1999) supported the idea of heritability.

A significant family connection has also been found with social phobia (Fyer et al, 1995; Stein et al, 1998), though it is difficult to separate the biological and environmental factors, as all will have experienced a similar environment. A multi-dimensional approach, which considers biological and environmental factors together, may work better.

Psychological explanations of phobia

Behavioural
The behavioural explanation of phobias is conditioning, both operant (where the fear is learnt through negative reinforcement) and classical (where the phobia is acquired through association). Both these suggest the person who becomes fearful of an object or situation has learned to do so through experience.

What may start as a low level of anxiety can escalate to a phobia by constant reinforcement of avoidance behaviour. For example, if a child is slightly fearful of dogs and the mother picks the child up every time there is a dog in the street, she is effectively reinforcing the fear.

The phobia can then be maintained by negative reinforcement, so when a person comes across a dog, they may cross the road, thus avoiding the dog. In the short term this relieves the anxiety, but in the long term maintains the phobia. Only when the person faces their fear directly will they be able to break the cycle of negative reinforcement and fear.

An example of classical conditioning can be seen in the Watson and Rayner (1920) study on Little Albert. Albert became fearful of rats after they were associated with a loud noise. He then actively escaped rats and other fluffy white things by turning away from them and protesting very loudly. This avoidance behaviour will have increased the fear to a phobia.

See also:
Approaches:
behavioural;
Conditioning:
classical;
Conditioning:
operant.

See also:
Disorders: OCD

Some phobias fit neatly into this explanation, such as a person experiencing a panic attack in their car, leading to a driving phobia (Munjack, 1984). However, there is a problem of reliability as the study by Watson and Raynor has never been successfully replicated - and it would now be ethically unacceptable to try to do so. In addition, there is no evidence that *all* phobia is caused by conditioning; not all people have a bad experience prior to developing a phobia (Ost, 1987).

In the case of a person with a phobia of dogs, behaviourists would assume there had probably been a traumatic experience with a dog. The associated distress is now felt with all dogs.

A social learning theory explanation would investigate whether the person is modelling their behaviour on someone they admire and therefore achieving attention for their fear, which will encourage the behaviour to recur.

See also: Social learning theory.

Cognitive
These explanations focus on the negative thought processes that can lead to anxiety. For example, when confronted with an ambiguous situation, an anxious

person is more likely to perceive it as a threat and assume there are going to be negative consequences, thus increasing anxiety levels (Mathews and MacLeod, 1994).

A socially-anxious person will be more concerned than most about how others see them and will be more aware of their self-image (Bates, 1990). They are also more likely to see themselves in a negative light, even when they contradict this thought process with good performance (Wallace and Alden, 1997). However, Twentyman and McFall (1975) found that socially-anxious people were more likely to have a low rating in social skills.

Cognitive-behaviour therapy has had some success in treating phobic patients, although cognitive explanations do not explain *how* negative thought processes develop.

Research: Bandura and Rosenthal (1966)

Bandura and Rosenthal (1966) had participants observe a role model (confederate) in a fearful situation, where the model was hooked up to a chair. When a buzzer sounded, the model appeared to be in a great deal of pain, pulling away from the chair rapidly. The participants' physiological responses were recorded and after several buzzer episodes, they showed increased levels of emotional response whenever the buzzer sounded. This demonstrated the participants had learnt to be fearful of the buzzer through the experience of the model (vicarious learning).

See also:
Approaches to psychology.

Therapies
Treatments for anxiety disorders vary according to the type of anxiety. For instance, if treating a specific phobia, such as fear of spiders, systematic desensitisation would be a behavioural treatment. This would involve creating a hierarchy of fear and meeting that fear over a series of systematic steps, until the fear levels are controllable by the client. Other therapies include psychotherapy from the

See also:
Therapies: behavioural.

psychodynamic approach and medication is also available to reduce the physiological symptoms of anxiety. The most effective treatment for phobias seems to be CBT, where the sufferer will be treated to perceive the feared thing differently and change their behaviour accordingly.

See also:
Therapies: CBT.

Case study: agoraphobia

Since Jenny's divorce, she has found it increasingly difficult to go out as she is fearful she will not be able to get back to safety. She has not been out for two months. Her symptoms include palpitations, sweats and hyperventilation if she attempts to go out. She appears to be suffering from agoraphobia.

From a biological perspective, Jenny's symptoms indicate there is probably a malfunction in the fight-or-flight response to danger, or that a biochemical imbalance is causing the excessive firing of arousal messages into her brain.

A psychodynamic explanation would suggest a traumatic event in childhood, such as being abused by one or both of her parents.

Behavioural explanations would focus on environmental factors, such as the impact of her relationship breakdown; perhaps her ex-husband was controlling and she had learnt to feel unable to cope when not being controlled.

A cognitive explanation would focus on her negative evaluation of situations, such as her life after divorce. Yet if Jenny also had a genetic predisposition toward irrational and negative thinking, this could have triggered her condition.

References

AYALA, E. S. et al (2009) Treatments for Blood-Injury-Injection Phobia: A Critical Review of Current Evidence. *Journal of Psychiatric Research*. 43 (15). pp.1235–42.

BATES, G. W. (1990) *Social Anxiety and Self-Presentation: Conversational Behaviours and Articulated Thought of Heterosexually Anxious Males*. Unpublished Doctoral Dissertation, University of Melbourne, Australia.

FYER, A. J. et al (1995) Specificity in Familial Aggregation of Phobic Disorders. *Archives of General Psychiatry*. 52. pp.564–73.

KESSLER, R. C. et al (1994) Lifetime and 12-Month Prevalence of DSM-III-R Psychiatric Disorders in the United States: Results from the National Comorbidity Survey. *Archives of General Psychiatry*. 51. pp.8–19.

LACEY, J. L. (1967) Somatic Response Patterning and Stress: Some Revisions of Activation Theory. In Appley, M. H. & Trumball, R. (Eds.), *Psychological stress*. New York: McGraw-Hill.

McNALLY, R. J. (1997) Atypical Phobias. In Davey, G. C. L. (Ed.) *Phobias: A Handbook of Theory, Research and Treatment*. pp.183–99. Chichester, UK: Wiley.

MUNJACK, D. J. (1984) The Onset of Driving Phobias: *Journal of Behaviour Therapy and Experimental Psychiatry*. 15. pp.305–8.

OST, L-G. (1987). Age of Onset in Different Phobias. *Journal of Abnormal Psychology*. 96. pp.223–9.

STEIN, M. B. et al (1998) A direct-Interview Family Study of Generalized Social Phobia. *American Journal of Psychiatry*. 155. pp.90–7

Disorders: schizophrenia

Schizophrenia is a psychotic disorder characterised by severe disruptions in psychological functioning and a loss of contact with reality. It covers a wide range of symptoms, which include hallucinations and delusions. It has been the subject of much research. There is even debate as to whether schizophrenia exists as a single disorder.

What is schizophrenia?

The term schizophrenia (literally meaning 'split mind') was first suggested by Eugen Bleuler's 1908 lecture, although the condition had been identified in the 19th century. In 1896, Emil Kraepelin defined it as a 'chronic deteriorating psychotic disorder'. It is generally accepted as a disorder that covers a variety of syndromes (recognisable symptoms that occur together). Kraepelin and Bleuler agreed that it involved cognitive disturbances, linked to behavioural symptoms and a neurological defect. From the start, then, this disorder was recognised as having biological characteristics and causes.

Schizophrenia is found in about 1% of the population and is more common in men than in women (Kirkbride et al, 2006). Onset is generally in adolescence or early adulthood, appearing earlier in men.

Symptoms of schizophrenia

Sufferers typically have a number of acute episodes of severe symptoms and will experience a less severe form of the symptoms between episodes. Around 30 years ago the symptoms were defined as:

➤ positive = additions or exaggerations of normal behaviour or thought processes

➤ negative = deficits of normal emotional responses or thought processes.

The diagram shows the range of positive and negative symptoms found in this disorder. Not all symptoms have to be present, but hallucination and/or delusions of some sort are two of the primary symptoms.

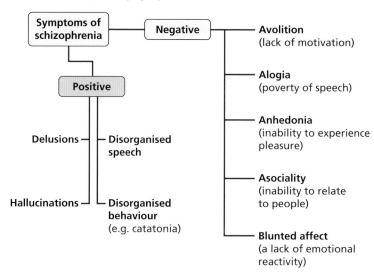

Diagnosis

The diagnostic criteria, according to the new DSM 5, are that two or more of the following symptoms must be present for at least one month, with signs of the disorder for at least six months, and that one symptom should be delusions, hallucinations or disorganised speech.

➤ Delusions

➤ Hallucinations

➤ Disorganised speech

➤ Abnormal psychomotor behaviour (e.g. catatonia)

➤ Negative symptoms

The level of function in the sufferer must also be noticeable, which means they have difficulties keeping a job, having relationships and caring for themselves.

DSM-5 has raised the symptom threshold, requiring that an individual exhibit at least two specified symptoms.

(In the previous edition, DSM-IV, the threshold was one.) Also, the diagnostic criteria no longer identify subtypes of schizophrenia defined by the predominant symptom at the time of evaluation. For example, in paranoid schizophrenia the main symptoms were hallucinations or delusions; in catatonic schizophrenia, the symptoms were movement abnormalities (e.g. flailing limbs about).

Explanation of schizophrenia

What causes schizophrenia remains a much debated area with theories focusing on different biological and psychological explanations. Most psychologists will agree that schizophrenia arises from a combination of factors.

Psychological explanations
Cognitive psychologists focus on the importance of disturbed thinking processes (as Kraepelin and Bleuler did), since people presenting with the disorder generally show abnormality in their thinking processes and the way they perceive things. Saccuzzo & Braff (1981) found that 'slow information processing' (not being able to think clearly and efficiently) on a regular basis was a characteristic of patients with schizophrenia in both severe and mild sufferers. In the milder sufferers, this deficit was reversible.

Some theories have suggested it is the home environment as a cause, i.e. being part of a 'schizo-phrenogenic family', where there is high emotional tension, lies and conspiracy, along with the 'double bind hypothesis' suggesting that mixed messages from parents, who are both doubting and complimentary, result in low self-esteem and confusion.

Biological explanations
There is a strong case for schizophrenia having a physical cause. Studies into genetics, e.g. McGiffen et al (1995), found that when a person has two schizophrenic parents there is a 50% chance of developing the disorder,

compared to an average risk of less than 1% in the general population. The Genain Quadruplets, an example of a shared predispostion for schizophrenia, all developed the disorder, (but they displayed different types of schizophrenia).

Schizophrenia is also thought to be caused by a biochemical imbalance, with dopamine being indicated as a cause for the hallucinations. Brain structure is also known to be different in most schizophrenics – most commonly they have enlarged ventricles in the brain – but it is not certain if the disorder is caused by this structure, or the structure is changed due to the disorder.

Environmental explanations
The biological evidence is extensive, but it is generally accepted that environment must also play a part, as living in densely populated areas shows a rise in the incidence of schizophrenia (Van Os J et al, 2003). Evidence also links cannabis use to the onset of schizophrenia.

References

BERRIAS, G. E. (2011) Eugen Bleuler's Place in History of Psychiatry. *Schizophrenia Bulletin*. 37 (6). pp.1095–8.

BLEULER, E. (1950) *Dementia Praecox or the Group of Schizophrenia*. New York: International universities Press (originally published 1911).

KIRKBRIDE, B. et al (2006) Heterogeneity in the Incidence of Schizophrenia and Other Psychotic Illnesses: Results from the 3-Center Aesop Study. *Archives of General Psychiatry*. 63. pp.250–8.

LINDSEY, S. J. E. & POWELL, G. E (1994) The Clinical Adult Psychology Handbook. 2nd Ed. London: Routledge.

SACUZZO, D. P. & BRAFF D. L. (1981) Early Information Processing Deficit in Schizophrenia. *Archives of General Psychiatry*. 38. pp.175–9.

VAN OS, J. et al (2003) *American Journal of Psychiatry*. 160. pp.477–82.

Issues: culture and gender bias

There is potential for bias (prejudice and preconceptions) in psychological theories and research. Culture bias exists when the researcher uses their own culture as a baseline for the way people should act, feel and think. Gender bias in psychology, which is also a form of culture bias, is mainly concerned with unfair and unwarranted assumptions toward women.

Culture bias

The two main types of culture bias are ethnocentrism and eurocentrism.

Ethnocentrism
This is where the psychologist uses their cultural norms as the standard to measure other cultures against. Such norms include the attitudes, beliefs and actions of that culture and in this case are seen as superior to norms of other cultures and sub cultures, such as race and gender.

Another aspect of ethnocentrism is the inappropriate generalising of research findings beyond the culture they were formed from. Most theory and research is derived from an individualistic perspective, but this may then be generalised to include how people should behave in collectivist cultures, where values are often quite different.

Eurocentrism
This relates to the fact that most psychological theories and research come from Europe and North America. The knowledge gained is then regarded as a universal description of behaviour. It does not assume superiority, as does ethnocentrism, but instead seems to ignore the differences.

Emic and etic approaches
Emic and etic show the two pathways cultural bias can take, as shown in the table opposite.

Emic	Etic
➤ The researcher only studies a phenomenon **within one culture**, though the results are then generalised to all other cultures.	➤ Research takes place outside of a specific culture.
➤ The findings are only really significant in that particular culture.	➤ Because several cultures are studied, findings may be considered to be universal. However, researchers will probably be from one specific culture, therefore bringing their own cultural values with them.
➤ The restrictive nature of this approach becomes a problem when evidence gained from a specific culture is generalised to other cultures out of the context in which the findings were found.	➤ Another problem is the lack of context in which the behaviour took place. Researchers will be unfamiliar with culture, which may cause bias.

Gender bias

Gender bias takes one of two pathways. This can have an impact on how research is carried out and consequently how it is interpreted.

➤ **Alpha bias** is where the differences between gender are exaggerated.

➤ **Beta bias** is where gender differences are ignored.

An example of alpha bias would be 'Androcentrism', where male behaviour is seen as the standard that all behaviour should be judged on. Female behaviour that strays from this ideal is seen as deviant.

An example of beta bias can be seen in Kohlberg's theory of moral development. His research design disadvantaged females, and this subsequently affected his assumptions – that females were morally deficient, which he took as being a consequence of their limited lives in the home (Kohlberg & Krammer, 1969). Follow-up studies, where gender bias was removed, showed Kohlberg's assumption to be wrong (Gablemen – Rupp, 1996).

Publishers of professional journals favour alpha bias when it comes to selecting work to be published (Travis, 1993). There appears to be more chance of work being published if there is a clear gender difference in the results, leading to a biased picture of what research is really showing.

Case Study: intelligence

Cultural variation, while evident in many areas of psychology, is highlighted in the areas of intelligence and relationships. Richard Nisbett (2003) argues that "East Asian and Western cultures have developed cognitive styles that differ in fundamental ways, including in how intelligence is understood." This presents a problem, as a global comparison of intelligence is impossible, and without an equal standard for comparing performance, it will be difficult to predict trends in needs and behaviour of societies.

Dealing with cultural bias in psychological research

Heterosexism is a form of bias, where opposite sex attraction and relationships are classed as the norm and other forms of sexuality and relationships are thought to be inferior, such as homosexuality. Historically, this type of bias also affected psychological research, with some studies dismissing or invalidating any form of orientation other than heterosexuality. In 1985 the APA's Board for Social and Ethical Responsibility in Psychology (BSERP) put together a task force to encourage non-homophobic research. From conception of an idea to be tested, through to interpretation and publication of psychological research, heterosexism was challenged. Prior to this intervention a review by Morin (1977) had found that sexuality other than heterosexuality was treated from a sickness model perspective, also reflected by the fact that the APA's DSM did not remove the status of homosexuality as a mental illness until 1975.

Bias free theory

Worrrell & Remer (1992) came up with the idea of how to avoid bias in psychological research against women, they came up with 4 criteria.

Gender free research, where sexist stereotyped ideas of females should be avoided

Flexibility, which was to accept all on an equal basis, with no assumptions of superiority or inferiority, but rather see each person as an individual

Interactionist where multiple factors are seen as influencing behaviour, of which gender might be one

Lifespan, which assumes behaviour is changeable and does not own a chronological age or have a gender. It is also suggests behaviour is not determined, but rather each individual has choices that may or may not be affected by the culture, history and environment of that person's lifespan

As is clear these can be adapted to other types of bias such as culture.

References

GABLEMAN-RUPP, L. (1996) "An analysis of adolescent male and female responses to Kohlberg's moral interview: Using two different editions of the Standard Issue Scoring Manual (1979 vs. 1987)". *Teaching and Leadership - Dissertations.* Paper 117. http://surface.syr.edu/tl_etd/117

GILLIGAN, C. (1982). *In a Different Voice.* Cambridge, MA: Harvard University Press.

KOHLBERG, L. & KRAMER, R. (1969) Continuities and Discontinuities in Childhood and Adult Moral Development. *Human Development.* 12. pp.93–120.

NISBETT, R. (2003) "The Geography of Thought" USA: Free Press.

TAVRIS, C. (1993) The Mismeasure of Women. *Feminism and Psychology.* 3 (2). pp.149–68.

WORELL, J. & REMER, P. (1992). Feminist Perspectives in Therapy: An Empowerment Model for Women. New York: John Wiley.

Issues: reductionism

Reductionism is when a complex event is reduced to a few components, in order to simplify it and so make it easier to understand. The debate as to whether reductionism should be used in studying the behaviour of people, is hotly contested. Some psychologist believe this approach to be fundamental; others that it is counter-productive. In order to understand the debate, it is necessary to know the different kinds of reductionism, and the different reductionist explanations.

Kinds of reductionism

According to Rose (1997) there are three kinds:

1. Experimental reductionism covers methods that simplify behaviour to isolated variables. Behaviour is often operationalised (see Research: reliability and validity: investigator effects) and then manipulated, creating an independent variable (IV). The effects of the difference or similarity in behaviour are measured from the IV, with the dependent variable (DV) being used to determine cause and effect.

2. Reductionism as an explanation or theory. The best 'principles' and 'laws' are often the simplest, for example the Yerkes-Dodson Law (1908) that there is an optimum level of anxiety for the best memory recall (too much or too little will negatively affect recall).

3. Reductionism in psychology as part of a philosophy, where the aim is to fit into other sciences easily: all sciences should be able to be reduced to a physical law.

While much scientific work in psychology has been valuable, some research has been limited in its real-life application. In the case of the laboratory experiments conducted by Elizabeth Loftus (1974) and several associates, breakthroughs were made as to why eye witness testimony (EWT) may be unreliable. However, there have been problems in the results translating to behaviour outside the laboratory. Yuille and Cutchell (1986) demonstrated this when their results were the opposite of Loftus's, showing there are more important variables than just the operationalised ones at work. This suggests experimental reductionism may cause the researcher to miss important aspects of behaviour, so reducing the value of the results in the understanding of human behaviour.

Reductionism in psychological research

Physiological reductionism
Behaviour is explained in terms of physical components, (biochemical interaction, genetics, brain structures and micro-organisms) and mechanisms, for example that certain types of behaviour, such as aggression or schizophrenia, are caused by action of neurotransmitters and hormones.

This approach has allowed for the development of drug therapy to treat the behaviours, and a more tolerant attitude to the behaviours as the 'blame' is removed.

However, the drugs can have devastating side effects, and reliance on drugs does mean other successful therapies, such as psychotherapy, may not be used.

Environmental reductionism
According to the behavioural approach, all behaviour results from a response to a stimulus in the environment. Environmental reductionism ignores innate influences not only for humans, but also for other animals. This can lead to particular ethical problems in research, if the idea exists that non-human animals have no cognition or emotions. Results found in other animals may also be generalised to humans. Social context and motivation are just two examples of factors that are not then accounted for.

See also:
Research: Using animals.

Machine reductionism
Machine reductionism is widely used in cognitive psychology, taking machine systems as an analogy of the information processing of the mind. An example of this is

Atkinson and Shifrin's multi-store model of memory, which breaks the process of memory into simple components to theorise how memory works. This type of reductionism has meant the development of memory theory is sustained by scientific evidence.

Gestalt psychologists, however, take a holistic approach, believing that humans are more complex entities that cannot be broken down into constituent parts. Indeed, the multi-store model of memory has now been overtaken by the interactionist idea that memory is developed through experiences, which are therefore peculiar to each person. An individual's memory depends on how a stimulus interacts with their experiences to date, which is contrary to the machinist idea.

See also:
Approaches:
humanist.

Arguments for and against reductionism

For reductionism	Against reductionism
If we all consist of a collection of the same atoms, it should be possible to explain behaviour by researching a small sample of those atoms.	Dualism (a separate mind and body) contradicts the idea that we can study the physical aspects of a person and understand their behaviour.
This assumes that behaviour is just the product of a sum of parts and there is no special life force, such as Freud's libido. There are no psychological events that are not caused by a physical reason. In other words, only what is physical matters when explaining behaviour (materialism).	For example, the power of the mind is capable of causing the same changes to serotonin and noradrenaline in depressed patients who are treated with psychotherapy alone, as depressed patients who have drug treatment (Martin et al, 2001).

For reductionism	Against reductionism
Reductionism is useful in understanding. For example, to find out how a bike works, you might take it apart then put it back together, or consider each component and then how all the components work together. In psychology we understand how stress works by looking at the interaction of the nervous system (ANS) and the endocrine system (hormones and neurotransmitters).	Reductionist methodology assumes the different parts of a person can be taken apart, studied, understood and then reconstructed like a jigsaw. Unfortunately humans are more complex than that and there will always be pieces missing from the jigsaw. This might explain why, after over a century, the problems of the mind are far from being solved.
It is useful to look at the reasons for behaviour on several levels. There are thought to be lower levels (looking at behaviour from a physical level) and higher levels, such as psychological (Rose, 1992). A compilation of all levels will contribute to a better understanding of behaviour.	Wolpe (1973) developed the behavioural therapy of systematic desensitisation. He used it on a patient with a fear of insects and found the therapy wasn't working because he was only treating her on a behavioural level (stimulus leading to response). In fact, her fear of insects turned out to reflect her marital problems, as her husband had an insect nickname. Wolpe recommended marriage counselling, which solved the problems. eliminating her phobia.

References

ATKINSON, R. C. & SHIFFRIN, R. M. (1968). "Chapter: Human Memory: A Proposed System and Its Control Processes". In SPENCE, K. W. & SPENCE, J. T. *The Psychology of Learning and Motivation* (Volume 2). pp.89–195. New York: Academic Press.

MARTIN, S. D. et al (2001) Brain Blood Flow Changes in Depressed Patients Treated with the Interpersonal Psychotherapy or Venlafaxine Hydrochloride. *Archives of General Psychiatry*. 58. pp.641–8.

ROSE, S. (1992) *The Making of Memory: From Molecule to Mind*. London, Bantam Books.

ROSE, S. (1997) *Lifelines*: Life Beyond the Gene. Oxford University Press.

WOLPE, J. (1973) *The Practice of Behaviour Therapy*. New York: Pergamon Press.

Memory: cognitive interview

The Cognitive Interview (CI) technique uses knowledge from psychological research into memory (e.g. reconstructive memory) to improve the accuracy in recall of events by witnesses and victims of crime. Developed as an alternative to the original police interview, it has been shown to produce more recall of events, along with a greater accuracy rate.

Theoretical ideas behind CI

Eyewitness testimony (EWT) is known to suffer from inaccuracy and distortion, for a variety of reasons, such as the process of reconstructive memory and from questions being asked in the wrong way. The CI is based on the assumption that there are several retrieval paths in memory (Tulving 1974). The CI therefore uses a number of strategies on the basis that if the memory is not available via one retrieval path, it may be available via another.

The second idea behind CI technique is Tulving & Thomson's encoding specificity theory (1973), which suggests that when we acquire memories we encode them with links to our current context and state. Hence, memory can be retrieved more successfully using cues or triggers about the context (features of the environment where the event took place) or about the person's state (how they were feeling inside when it happened).

See also: Memory: reconstructive.

CI also makes confabulation less likely, where gaps in the memory are filled in with information the person believes to be true, but is in fact false. In other words, there is less likelihood of memory reconstructing Itself.

See also: Eye witness testimony.

Cognitive Interview technique

Four main techniques are used in CI. These form the basis for the Cognitive Interview Schedule developed by Geiselman et al. (1985) and used by police investigators:

1. **Hypermnesia** – recalling everything, no matter how small, on the basis that remembering small things can trigger recall of bigger events.

2. **Change of narrative order** – recalling things out of chronological order. Witnesses may be asked to remember the most memorable part of the event and work backwards, or start from the last thing they remember to the beginning of the event. This aims to reduce the possibility of gaps in the information, in other words, it decreases the possibility of reconstructive memory happening.

3. **Mental reinstatement of context** – being asked to remember things about the environment, such as the weather and features of the place where the event took place. Witnesses will also be asked what their emotional state was at the time of the event.

4. **Change of perspective** – being asked to give an account of the event from another viewpoint, such as the person who was standing close by. This also aims to reduce the effects of reconstructive memory.

After the interview, an audio recording will be analysed and other material, such as drawings, will be vital to put what is said in the recordings into context. The transcript that has been made of the interview needs to be written up in the third person, to show it is a reconstructed account of what was said. The draft should ideally be shown to the witness  to approve and to check whether the interviewer's interpretation is correct or needs to be clarified.

Case study: crime witness

Charlie is witness to a shop robbery at gunpoint, so later the police question him. Firstly they ask him to recall all he remembers, no matter how insignificant he thought it was (hypermnesia). The police ask Charlie if he can remember where he was in the shop, what he could see and how he felt (mental reinstatement of context). They then ask him if there were any other people in the shop and what he thought they would have seen (change of perspective). Finally, they ask him to go over what he saw, from the most memorable event and work backwards (change of narrative order).

Enhanced cognitive interview

An 'enhanced' cognitive interview has been developed (Bekerian & Dennett 1993) that uses the same format as described above, but also encourages rapport building between interviewer and interviewee. It is also made clear to the interviewee that the interviewer has no knowledge of the incident. This means there is no prompting and the statement is all the witness's work.

Research: Fisher *et al* (1989)

This study tested the validity of the enhanced CI with witnesses to mugging and shoplifting in Miami. They compared the testimony gathered using the enhanced CI and the standard interview. They found there were 47% more relevant facts gained in the enhanced CI group.

Bekerian and Dennett (1993) reviewed 27 studies using the Cognitive Interview technique and found that in all cases it helped elicit more accurate information than other interview procedures.

The reliability and validity of CI continues to be supported by research, but has also withstood the test of criminal court trials. Research has also compared CI to standard interview technique and has proven more effective on each occasion. Fisher et al (2000) asked whether recall using CI was as good after a long time period and found it to be effective even 35 years after an event. Milne & Bull (2006) found that CI was also more effective in people with learning disabilities and children, in comparison to a standard interview.

References

BEKERIAN, D. A. & DENNETT, J. L. (1993) The Cognitive Interview Technique: Reviving the Issues. *Applied Cogntive Psychology*. 7. pp.275–97.

FISHER, R. P. GIESELMAN, R. E. & AMADOR, M. (1989) Field Test of the Cognitive Interview: Enhancing the Recollection of Actual Victims and Witnesses of Crime. *Journal of Applied Psychology*. 74. pp.722–7.

FISHER, R. P. et al (2000), Adapting the Cognitive Interview to Enhance Long Term Recall of Physical Activities. *Journal of Applied Psychology*. 85. pp.180–9.

GEISELMAN, R. E. et al (1985) Enhancement of Eyewitness Testimony with the Cognitive Intervie. *American Journal of Psychology*. 99. pp.385–401.

MILNE, R. & BULL, R. (2006) Interviewing Victims of Crime, Including Children and People with Intellectual Disabilities. In Kebbrell, M. & Davies, G. (eds.). *Practical Psychology for Forensic Investigations and Prosecutions*. pp.7–24. Chichester, UK: Wiley.

TULVING, E. & THOMSON, D. M. (1973) Encoding Specificity and Retrieval Processes in Episodic Memory. *Psychological Review*. 80. pp.352–73.

Memory: eye witness testimony

Eye witness testimony (EWT) links the theories of memory to everyday life and is mainly concerned with investigation into factors that affect accuracy, such as leading questions, anxiety and age. An eyewitness is a person who witnesses an event as a victim or a bystander. The testimony (an account of what the person saw or heard) contributes to a police investigation and possibly testimony given in court.

The main issue when considering eye witness testimony is how reliable and accurate it is, as in the past innocent people have spent time in prison due to unreliable witness statements. Elizabeth Loftus has been a key researcher in this area, focusing mainly on the effect of post-event information, or misinformation. As well as reconstructive memory, research into looking at the effects of anxiety and age on eye witness testimony is a growth area.

See also:
Memory:
reconstructive.

Leading questions

Research suggests that the way a witness is questioned has a significant influence on the accuracy of testimony, particularly when leading questions are used. Leading questions are those that imply or insinuate a situation and can be as simple as changing a verb in a question (see Research). Leading questions, or misinformation as Loftus now refers to it, cause errors in what appears to be unstable memory of an event, these errors then become part of the memory. Loftus calls this 'misinformation acceptance'.

This has serious implications for how a witness is questioned, which is why the cognitive interview was developed. Misinformation serves to transform the memory by removing some elements and causing others to be inserted. However, the leading questions research carried out by Loftus and colleagues has all been laboratory based, therefore the results gained cannot necessarily be generalised to a real-life situation.

See also:
Cognitive
interview.

The effect of anxiety

Loftus also investigated the effects of anxiety on EWT accuracy, primarily with her weapon effect study. It showed that witness focus can be disturbed by causes of anxiety, such as a knife, making EWT incomplete and inaccurate.

However, a conflicting view on the effect of anxiety and memory is the Yerkes-Dodson effect (1908), which suggests there is an optimum level of anxiety, where detail and memory accuracy is at its peak.

In support of the Yerkes-Dodson effect, Christianson & Hubinette (1993) carried out a survey on 110 people who witnessed bank robberies and found the people who had been threatened directly (therefore at the highest anxiety level) had much better recall in detail and accuracy than those who had been bystanders.

It would appear that the results of studies carried out in real-life situations show an opposing outcome to the laboratory studies of Loftus. For one thing, real life studies are more easily generalised to what would actually happen in a situation, and so have high ecological validity.

It would seem that when there is an optimum level of anxiety, the memory becomes less fragile and less prone to being distorted or confused.

Age and accuracy

Age is another important influence on EWT accuracy. Studies of a full range of ages have found that, in general, the very young and very old are the most inaccurate:

➤ Parker & Carranza (1989) found that primary school children were more likely to select someone from an identification line-up, compared to college students, but were generally more inaccurate.

➤ Children are more likely to accept inaccurate information from adults and will not generally contradict them if they wrongly interpret what the child had said. This suggests that children are more susceptible to leading questions. Alternatively, as children have not had as much time to develop their schema, they are more likely to say exactly what they saw if they only respond to a question once.

➤ Studies such as Mermon et al (2003) have shown that older adults tend to perform worse in EWT research.

➤ Research into own-age bias suggests we are more accurate at identifying people in a similar age bracket to ourselves. As much of the research involved participants identifying younger adults, it is not surprising that older adults proved not as accurate.

➤ Similarly, own-race bias suggests we can identify people from our own ethnic background better than those from another, particularly when there are significant differences in features (Brigham & Malpass, 1985).

Research: Loftus and Palmer (1974)

The researchers asked student groups to watch a video of several car accidents. They then asked a critical question about the speed: 'How fast were the cars going when they ...'. For each group the verb was different, either *hit, smashed, collided, bumped* or *contacted*. They found that the question with the most intense verb (*smashed*) elicited the highest estimate of speed. The lowest estimate of speed was *contacted*.

There were two possible reasons for the results gained:

1. Participants were simply reacting to the difference in verb.

2. Their perception of the accident had changed due to the way the question was asked (leading question).

To discover the more likely reason, Loftus and Palmer did a second experiment. This used a new set of participants who watched an accident video for a short period and were then put into three conditions: 50 were given the *smashed* question, 50 *hit,* and the rest were a control group not given a leading question. The results confirmed an increase in speed when the verb *smashed* was used.

A week later, the same participants were given post-event information (information given after the event they had already commented on). They were asked, 'Did you see any broken glass on the road?' (There was none.) Those who had been in the *smashed* group were twice as likely to say there was glass, compared to the *hit* group. There had been a change in perception of the accident witnessed as a result of the original leading question, when asked about estimation of speed. The implications of these findings were enormous and changed the way witnesses and victims are now questioned (the cognitive interview technique).

Case study

Sarah was nine when she witnessed her mother being stabbed to death but could not recall details of the murderer until years later. Loftus would explain it as experiencing too much anxiety, causing a negative effect on recall and making the testimony unreliable. Conversely, the Yerkes Dodson law would explain this as being due to extreme anxiety, but as the emotions were worked through, Sarah could then recall effectively. So the testimony is not unreliable, just difficult to access.

References

BRIGHAM, J. C. & MALPASS, R. S. (1985) The Role of Experience and Contact in the Recognition of Faces of Own-Other-Race Persons. *Journal of Social Issues*. 41 (3). pp.139–55.

LOFTUS, E. F., LOFTUS, G. R. & MESSO, J. (1987) Some Facts About 'Weapon Focus'. *Law and Human behaviour*. 11. pp.55–62.

LOFTUS, E. F. & PALMER, J. C. (1974) Reconstruction of Automobile Destruction: An Example of the Interaction Between Language and Memory. *Journal of Verbal Learning and Verbal Behaviour*. 13. pp.585–9.

MERMON, A. et al (2003) Exposure Duration: Effects on Eyewitness. Accuracy and Confidence. *British Journal of Psychology*. 94. pp.339–54.

PARKER, J. F. & CARRANZA, L. E. (1989) Eyewitness Testimony of Children in Target-Present and Target-Absent Line-Ups. *Law and Human Behaviour*. 13. pp.133–49.

Memory: forgetting

Forgetting is the term used when information cannot be recalled. Forgetting can happen in both long-term memory (LTM) and short-term memory (STM). Reasons may include problems with availability, accessibility and interference. Explanations of forgetting use the ideas of memory processing.

Forgetting in STM

There are two main explanations for forgetting in STM: decay and displacement (both availability explanations).

Decay

This occurs when a memory trace disappears due to lack of attention to and/or rehearsal of the information being processed. If information is only encoded visually, for instance, there is little chance of a memory surviving without attention: if a car hits you and drives off quickly, it will be very hard to remember the registration number without verbalising it and continuously rehearsing it, especially as you would probably be paying more attention to your injury.

Displacement

There is only a certain amount of room in STM (7 ± 2 items – Miller 1956) and so only a certain amount of information can be retained until it is either transferred to LTM via attention and rehearsal or it is displaced. Old information is effectively written over by new information when the capacity of the store is full.

Research into forgetting in STM

Peterson & Peterson's study (1959) into the duration of STM can be seen as support for either decay or displacement. Participants were asked to recall a nonsense trigram (three random letters) after several time lapses, ranging from 3 to 18 seconds. During the time lapses they had to count back from a large three-digit number in 3s or 4s. This counting stopped participants rehearsing the trigram. The findings showed a 90% recall of the trigram after 3 seconds, but this declined sharply to 2% recall after 18 seconds. They concluded STM only lasted up to 18 seconds without rehearsal.

It is not clear whether the lack of memory was due to decay or displacement. Decay could have occurred because the trigram was not being attended to, so the trace just vanished. Alternatively, displacement could have occurred, because the amount of information participants had to process (in counting backwards) could have easily used up the limited capacity of STM, and so the older material (the trigram) was lost.

Forgetting in LTM

Decay in LTM

Decay in LTM means the memory was there in the past to retrieve, but has since disappeared through lack of use – in other words: if you don't use it, you lose it. It is thought this type of memory loss could be due to physical decay of the brain. Support for this idea comes from the fact that people who have disease such as dementia or who are brain damaged lose memories through lack of functioning. However, this doesn't explain why some people can remember information they have not used for a long time.

Trace decay in LTM is different from trace decay in STM, where the information disappears through lack of attention and rehearsal. Once in LTM, information is only stored and not processed, so it can be unattended for a period of time, leading to inaccessibility, neglect and deterioration.

Interference in LTM

Interference occurs when old and new memories interfere with each other. There are two types of interference:

➤ Proactive interference (PI): where past knowledge interferes with attempts to learn new knowledge. For example, you change phones and need to learn a new number, but the old number interferes with being able to memorise the new one.

➤ Retroactive interference (RI): where new knowledge interferes with old knowledge. Having memorised your new number, you then find it hard to remember the old number correctly.

Either type of interference can lead to knowledge becoming mixed up and the memory failing. Research by Underwood (1957) found evidence of proactive interference, while Tulving & Psotka (1971) found evidence of retroactive interference.

Cue dependency

Failure to retrieve information might be due to lack of access; in other words, the memory is there, but it needs the right trigger or cue to be activated. This could involve:

➤ Context dependency – in order to remember something, you mentally put it where it belongs. For example, if you have lost your keys, you might think about the last time you used them and retrace your steps.

➤ State dependency – this time the cue to recall is being in the same psychological or physical state. Miles & Hardman (1998) had participants either ride exercise bikes or rest while learning and recalling words; they found exercise made significant improvements on their recall when used as a state dependent cue.

Research into cue dependency includes the study by Tulving and Pearlstone (1966), which was the basis for Thomson & Tulving's (1970) 'encoding specificity principle'. This suggests that when we make memories, they are embedded in the context and so encoded together. Therefore, we find it easier to recall them if we are in a similar context.

See also:
Cognitive
interview.

Research: Godden and Baddeley (1975)

These researchers investigated whether learning and recalling words in the same or different place (context) had an impact on the amount of words remembered. They used divers and had them either under water or on land, which will have also affected their state. The results showed that when the divers learnt and recalled in different environments, their word recall was worse than If they learnt and recalled In the same environment. As there was a change of state for them, being underwater and using breathing equipment or on land breathing normally, the results also showed it was better to be in the same state when learning and recalling the words.

Emotional explanations of forgetting

Flashbulb memories

These occur when there is an intensely emotional event, such as a major tragedy (e.g. the 9/11 twin towers attacks in New York). People are able to remember what they were doing, the conversations they were having and so on. The memories are very detailed, as if a picture had been taken of the event. Although vivid and rich in content, the accuracy of the memories is questionable after long periods of time, as research shows them to have decay and be lacking in endurance (Schmolck et al, 2000).

Neisser (1982) suggests flashbulb memories are more like markers in a person's life rather than sustainable memories. Memorable incidents such as 9/11 mark events that cause big changes and so are remembered as turning points in life. Though details seem vivid, they may even be incorrect, as Neisser found from his personal experience.

Repression

Repression is an ego defence mechanism that makes it possible for the person to continue to function normally when they have suffered an unacceptable traumatic event. The memory of an event may go directly into the unconscious, to protect the conscious mind (ego). It does not disappear, but simply becomes inaccessible.

Herman & Schatzow (1987) studied 53 women who had been victims of incestuous violent abuse and found that 28% of them had at some point experienced severe memory deficits. Only after they took part in a short-term treatment group were the buried memories recovered.

See also:
Approaches:
psychodynamic.

References

ATKINSON, R. C. & SHIFFRIN, R. M. (1968) Human Memory: A Proposed System and Its Control Processes. In SPENCE, K. W. & SPENCE, J. T. (eds.) *The Psychology of Learning and Motivation*. Vol. 2. London: Academic Press.

BADDELEY, A. D. & HITCH, G. (1974). Working Memory. In BOWER, G. H. (ed.). *The Psychology of Learning and Motivation: Advances In Research And Theory*. New York: Academic Press.

HERMAN, J. L. & SCHATZOW, E. (1987) Recovery and Verification of Memories of Childhood Sexual Trauma. *Psychoanalytic Psychology*. 4. pp.1–14.

Memory: levels of processing

Levels of processing is a key concept in the study of memory. The idea was introduced by Craik and Lockhart (1972), who believed that stimuli are processed through a series of levels that become progressively more complex. They saw memory as the by-product of the processing of information: how long the memory lasts depends on how deeply the information is processed.

Depth of processing

Craik and Lockhart felt the key to enduring memory was the depth of processing.

➤ The simplest level is orthographic (visual) or shallow processing: this means processing material by the surface features of the stimuli, e.g. the shape of an image, such as the look of a word.

➤ The next, deeper level is phonetic (auditory), which means processing material from the sound. For example, when you are given a telephone number to remember, you will go over the numbers verbally and try and give them a verbal pattern of some sort.

➤ The deepest levels of processing (semantic, i.e. relating to meaning) will use complex strategies, such as elaborative rehearsal (thinking about the meaning of the method to be recalled, as opposed to simply repeating it).

For Craik and Lockhart, the key to long-lasting memory is the meaningfulness connected to stimuli. Strategies for improving memory should focus on the deepest level of processing.

Primary memory

Craik and Lockhart suggested that memory was produced in two ways: first, through a process of deep encoding, which results in enduring memories, and second, through a process they called 'recirculation'.

They felt recirculation was a lower level of processing and they called this 'primary memory' (a similar idea to short-term memory). They pointed out, though, that primary memory was different from STM, because rather than being limited static store (which is how models of memory tended to view STM), primary memory was more like a flexible central processor that retained information as long as it was being attended to in some way.

The generation effect

The generation effect suggests that we remember items better if we generate the items ourselves rather than studying items produced by others.

Research: semantic processing (Craik & Tulving)

Craik & Tulving (1975) carried out an experiment to see whether words that were processed with their meaning would be better remembered than words just processed for their appearance or sound. Participants were given a list of 40 one- or two-syllable words and were asked whether some words were in capitals (shallow), whether some words rhymed with another word (phonetic), or whether a word was part of a category or fitted a gap in a sentence (semantic). The participants simply had to answer yes or no to each question. The results showed that words that had been semantically processed were best remembered: 96% of words in the gap-filling question, compared to 18% of words recognised after shallow processing.

Implications for studying

When learning a subject at college, if students simply scan a handout and do nothing else with it (shallow processing), they will barely remember anything of what is on it. If they read the handout (phonetic), they will remember some of what is on it, but if they rewrite it into their own style and paraphrase it (semantic), they will remember more of it. For this reason it is better for handouts to have parts for students to fill in, so that they have to consider and summarise information.

Evaluation of the levels of processing model

Strengths

➤ The levels of processing model provides a convincing explanation of why we remember some things better and for longer than others.

➤ Craik and Lockhart's ideas stimulated much research in the field of memory and challenged the idea that memory is simply a kind of storage system.

Weaknesses

➤ The model has been described as more of a description than an explanation, as it does not explain *how* the deeper processing results in better memories.

➤ The concept of depth is vague and cannot be observed; it cannot be objectively measured.

References

CRAIK, F. I. M & LOCKHART, B. (1972) Levels of Processing. *Journal of Verbal Learning and Verbal Behaviour*. 11. pp.671–84.

CRAIK, F. I. M. & TULVING, E. (1975) Depth of Processing and Retention of Words in Episodic Memory. *Journal of Experimental Psychology*. 104. pp.268–94.

Memory: reconstructive

Reconstructive theory was introduced by Bartlett (1932) and is about the nature of long term memory (LTM), which he suggested was not static, but rather an ongoing process. He found that LTM was prone to 'imaginative reconstruction' and was affected by our knowledge of the world (expressed in terms of Schema), particularly when there were gaps in the memory.

Development of Bartlett's idea

Bartlett's theory was considered vague. In the 1970s, however, researchers interested in computer intelligence decided to refine the concept. In 1977, Schank & Abelson suggested that we acquire schemas for commonly experienced structured events. They used several events in their research, one of which was going to a restaurant. This involves certain expectations about what is going to happen (being seated at a table, choosing from a menu, ordering from a waiter, etc.), which ensure that we know what to do next.

Schemas

Schemas (also called 'schemata') are our knowledge of the world, built into frameworks to help us make sense of it. They help us to interpret new information and control our thoughts and actions. Schemas are key to many areas of cognitive psychology, especially memory processing and recall.

Rumelhart & Norman (1983) developed a five-point theory of how schemas affect memory:

1. Schemas represent knowledge, from simple to complex.

2. Schemas connect to form systems, also called scripts.

3. Schemas can contain a combination of different values:

   ➤ fixed values (characteristics that never change with all people – e.g. a doctor's office is where you sit and wait to be seen)

   ➤ optional values (features that change according to personal experience – e.g. a dentist's waiting room is terrifying to some people but not to others)

   ➤ default values (most typical characteristics in a given schema – e.g. you would expect a book to be on a shelf and not on the floor).

4. The content of schemas is developed through a combination of personal experience, culture and the assumptions people make, such as stereotyping.

5. All schemas have 'active recognition devices', i.e. we constantly use them to make sense of the world, by fitting new stimuli into the most appropriate place.

Schemas in eye witness testimony

Schema theory is particularly relevant to eye witness testimony. It seeks to explain how the use of schemas can easily cause errors in recall. Research was carried out by Brewer & Treyens (1981), who set up a room to resemble an office and put 61 different objects in the room. Most of the objects were what would be expected in an office, such as a typewriter, but there were also objects that were out of place, e.g. a skull. They left participants in the room for 35 seconds and afterwards asked them to recall the objects in the room. The most unusual objects were often accurately recalled; errors were made, however, as participants attempted to use office schemas, e.g. recalling books even though there were none.

If schemas are a mental shortcut to aid our understanding of new material quickly, they are often used with stereotyping. When a person witnesses a crime, they will use both of these (schemas and stereotyping) to help them build a story of what they saw. Therefore EWT is simply a person's view of what happened according to their past knowledge and expectations. That is why the development of the cognitive interview technique is so important.

See also:
Eye witness
testimony.

Research: the 'War of the Ghosts' study

Bartlett's (1932) 'War of the Ghosts' study tested his idea about reconstructive memory and was used as evidence, when he presented his concept to his peers. He used a South American folk tale, 'The War of the Ghosts', from the time when there was little knowledge of the outside world. He told the story to his British students, knowing that the story itself, and some of the word and phrases it contained, would not be known to them. He then asked students to recall the story, in words and pictures, on a number of occasions, by recalling their own or someone else's version of the story. This was called 'serial reproduction'.

He found his participants had cut the story drastically and that it had been affected by their knowledge of the world (schema). They had given it a meaning familiar to them and had used word from their culture, such as boats instead of canoes. The story's meaning had become distorted.

The study was criticised for lacking experimental controls, but many recent studies have been done with controls in place and gave the same results, that schemas affect memory.

References

BARTLETT, F. C. (1932) *Remembering*. Cambridge University Press.

BREWER, W. F. & TREYENS, J. C. (1981) Role of Schemata in Memory for Places. *Cognitive Psychology*. 13. pp.207–30.

RUMELHART, D. E. & NORMAN, D. A. (1983) Representation in Memory. In ATKINSON, R. C. HERNSTEIN, R. J. LINDZEY, B. & LUCE, R. D. (eds.) *Handbook of Experimental Psychology*. Chichester, UK: Wiley.

SCHANK, R. C. & ABELSON, R. (1977) *Scripts, Plans, Goals and Understanding*. Hillsdale, NJ: Lawrence Erlbaum Associates.

Memory: structure

Memory is an essential part of how the human mind processes information. As memory is a very large subject area, research into memory has tended to focus on small areas of study. In order to focus research, psychologists have defined the components of the memory (structure) and how those components process information (models). These are based on an analogy between the human mind and a computer (information processor).

Structure of memory

It is agreed by many that the memory process is made up of three main components: encoding, storage and retrieval (see figure). It is also accepted that memory consists of both long-term memory (LTM) and short-term memory (STM) storage units.

Basic components of memory

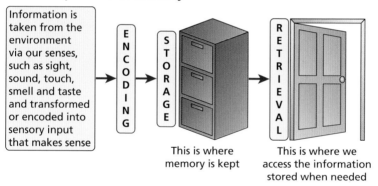

Information is taken from the environment via our senses, such as sight, sound, touch, smell and taste and transformed or encoded into sensory input that makes sense

This is where memory is kept

This is where we access the information stored when needed

➤ Encoding – information received through the senses is transformed into a chemical memory trace (an 'engrem') which will make sense. It then transfers to ...

➤ Storage – as a result of the encoding, it is stored in the memory system, a bit like filing a document until it is needed.

➤ Retrieval – recovering the stored information from the system. This is known as recall, or remembering.

Psychologists interested in the learning aspect of memory will focus on encoding and storage process. Those interested in pure memory will focus on the retrieval process. However, these processes are interdependent.

To give an everyday example, when students are learning in a class, they will first encode the information being given to them in a variety of ways, such as visually (by sight), acoustically (via hearing) and semantically (via meaning). These are the three main ways in which information is encoded. The information is then stored until it is needed – for example, to respond to a teacher's question about a topic just introduced (where information might be accessed from STM) or a topic covered earlier in the lesson (which might be accessed from LTM).

STM and LTM

The table opposite shows the key points of comparison between the processing features of STM and LTM, with the key pieces of research in some of the most common areas of interest.

	STM (Short-term memory)	LTM (Long-term memory)
Encoding (how the brain makes sense of sensory input)	Encoding is mainly acoustic (sound), but can also be visual Research: Baddley 1966, who did a study looking at encoding in both STM & LTM	Encoding is mainly semantic (meaning) Research: Baddley 1966, who did a study looking at encoding in both STM & LTM
Storage	Storage is temporary	Storage is thought to be permanent
Capacity (how much can be stored)	Limited to 5–9 items. Can be extended by using chunking (a process whereby several pieces of information, such as letters in a word, can be taken as one item) Research: Miller (1956) using the immediate digit span test	Capacity is thought to be unlimited
Duration (how long it can be stored)	Limited to 18–30 seconds if rehearsal is prevented, or up to 3 minutes if the person is free to rehearse the information Research: Study of immediate memory span by Baddeley et al (1975)	Duration is thought to be unlimited Research: Bahrick et al (1975), who studied memory over a 50-year span and named LTM as VLTM

Research evaluation

Apart from the research study by Bahrick et al (1975), the studies above share the same strengths and weaknesses.

Strengths

➤ The studies were carried out in laboratory conditions, so were highly controlled and had experimental validity.

➤ All the studies have been repeated and produced similar results, so can be said to have good reliability.

➤ As they use the hypothetico-deductive method (formulating the hypothesis before the study and testing it, rather than forming the hypothesis after the research has taken place), all studies were scientific and therefore could be trusted.

Weaknesses

➤ Mundane realism: the tasks participants were asked to do were not really representative of every-day tasks, and so it is questionable whether the same behaviour would occur in everyday and more important tasks.

➤ The studies lack ecological validity, as they took place in highly controlled environments which may have affected how participants reacted. This makes the results difficult to generalise to how people would act in a more natural environment.

Bahrick et al (1975)

This study had mundane realism and ecological validity, as people were being asked to recall old school friends and acquaintances. The results showed recall after 47 years was up to 70% if there was a cue, such as a name, which reduced to 30% recall if there was no cue. This showed memories can last for a very long time and can be retrieved well when helped along with a trigger.

A key problem with the study was whether the results were due to the duration of memory, or to other extraneous variables (factors that are present, but are not measured for and could have an effect on behaviour). These factors included the fact that participants knew they were going to meet at their old school and so may have looked at old yearbooks prior to going to the school. The memories would then not have been held over a period of years, but rather be from recent reminders. Many of the participants may also have stayed in touch, or live near the people they were asked to recall.

Models of memory

A model of memory is a way of representing or explaining how the process of memory works. There are three main models most common to students of psychology:

➤ **Multi-store model** as proposed by Atkinson and Shiffrin (1968) – this explained memory in terms of a linear flow of information through a series of fixed stages, with separate short-term and long-term stores.

➤ **Working memory model** (Baddeley and Hitch 1974) – it regards STM as a more flexible and complex system able both to store information and actively process it. It allows for a more complex encoding process than the multi-store model, though in its original form it only concentrated on short-term memory. This model has gone on to be developed by Baddeley into the multi-component model of memory.

➤ **Levels of processing** – Craik and Lockhart (1972) viewed memory slightly differently from the other two models. They saw memory as a by-product (not a main product) of information processing. The more deeply processed the information, the more likelihood of a good memory of it.

See also:
Memory: levels of processing;
Memory: reconstructive.

References

BERNSTEIN, D. A. et al (2000) *Psychology*. 5th Ed. New York: Houghton Mifflin.

ATKINSON, R. C. & SHIFFRIN, R. M. (1968) Human Memory: A Proposed System and Its Control Processes. In SPENCE, K. W. & SPENCE, J. T. (eds.) *The Psychology of Learning and Motivation*. Vol. 2. London: Academic Press.

BADDELEY, A. D. & HITCH, G. (1974) Working Memory. In Bower, G.H. (ed.) *The Psychology of Learning and Motivation*. Vol. 8. London: Academic Press.

Obedience

Obedience is a form of social influence, changing behaviour by a direct command or order. Psychologists are interested in the factors that cause people to obey or disobey. These include situational factors (to do with the circumstances the person finds themselves in when orders are given) and dispositional factors (factors that are unique to the individual being ordered, such as personality traits).

Situational factors

Legitimate authority figure

The presence of a person who has authority in a given context is more likely to get people to obey. There is much evidence to support this, including the Milgram study (1963), where a man in a lab coat was perceived as having authority in a laboratory situation. The prestige of the location added to his authority rating.

It was supported by later studies when an authority figure was not present and the obedience declined rapidly to 20.5%. Studies by Bickman (1974) and Hofling et al (1966) when nurses were told to administer what could have been a lethal dose of a drug they had no knowledge of by a doctor (legitimate authority figure) over the phone. The findings were shocking, with 98% of the nurses willing to obey this order without question, demonstrating the power of the legitimate authority figure.

Role of buffers

Buffers are factors that stop the person feeling the effects of their actions. For example, if a group of people were ordered to commit murder and given the choice to shoot the victim with a gun, stab them with a knife or strangle them by hand, most would prefer the gun. This is because there are several buffers including the gun itself, the bullet and the distance they can be away from the victim.

In the first Milgram experiment, there were several buffers, such as placing a wall between the 'learner' being given shocks and the teacher operating the equipment. In later studies, when buffers were gradually stripped away, the obedience also declined drastically, e.g. when the teacher had to place the learner's hand on the shock plate, obedience declined to 30%.

Gradual commitment
This relies on giving small inducements to commit more in small regular doses. In the Milgram study, participants were told to give a 15-volt shock at first and increase it by 15 volts each time. They will have become adjusted to giving electric shocks and in their mind the gradual 15-volt increases would not seem much. By the time they realised they were giving 100s of volts, they would have felt committed to continue.

Presence of allies
The presence of an ally can increase or decrease obedience, depending on what the ally is doing. If the ally obeys, the obedience rate will rise dramatically; if they disobey, the obedience rate will drop dramatically. In the Milgram experiment, when the ally obeyed, the learner's obedience rose to 92.5% and when the ally disobeyed it fell to 10%, so showing how potent social influence can be.

Dispositional factors

Locus of control
Rotter (1966) put forward the theory of locus of control. 'Locus' simply means place, so this is about where a person feels control over them lies.

➤ People with a high internal locus of control feel they mostly have control over their life; they are less likely to obey if they see an order as wrong, being confident that their abilities and input are what is needed to produce an outcome. They are also less likely to be swayed by society and so more likely to disobey or question orders.

➤ A person with high external locus of control feels they have little control over their own life, putting experiences and outcomes down to chance or luck. They much more likely to obey without question and to shift into an agentic state (see Agency theory below).

Rotter viewed locus of control as a continuum and suggested that either extreme would not be healthy.

Authoritarian personality
According to Adorno et al (1950) this type of personality has a high respect for the rules, whether right or wrong, and believes only complete obedience is acceptable. He introduced the F-scale to assess whether a person had an authoritarian personality – if a person scores 80 or more on the scale, they have a very high likelihood of obeying blindly, as they find it difficult to think for themselves.

Agency theory
Milgram (1974) suggested that people act somewhere between two extreme levels depending on both situation and disposition:

➤ Autonomous state – A person will behave independently, aware of the consequences of their actions and happy to take responsibility for their actions. This is more likely to be a person with high internal locus of control.

➤ Agentic state – A person who shifts into agentic state, (acts as an agent for another) and takes no responsibility for the consequences of their actions is more likely to have a higher external locus of control, believing they should obey someone they see as having more power than they do.

Milgram argueed that the social system leads a person into obedience by taking control of that person. The more the person becomes embedded into the agentic end of the spectrum, the more likely they are to obey without question. Milgram suggested the reason why people obey initially is due to early socialisation and training, but felt there were two key factors that enforced obedience in some: fear of being disliked or not fitting in with what society expects, and fear of increasing personal levels of anxiety, so obeying for a quiet life. The first is a very real fear as it can affect a person's standing, such as in a career.

Research: Milgram

Milgram wanted to know if ordinary Americans would obey an order to seriously harm another person. On arrival at Yale University, the participants entered the laboratory to the researcher in a lab coat (authority figure) and another middle aged man, who appeared to them as another participant, but was really a confederate (a person working for the researcher), called Mr Wallace. Both were supposedly picked at random to be either the learner or the teacher. The real participant was always the teacher.

The researcher in a lab coat explained to the men that every time the learner got an answer incorrect, the teacher would have to apply an electric shock, starting at 15 volts and increasing by 15 volts each time a question was incorrect. (There were no real shocks given.)

The findings showed that 100% of participants were willing to shock up to 300 volts and 65% willing to go all the way up to 450 volts, though some participants on several occasions expressed a wish to stop; the researcher insisted they continue.

The conclusion was that ordinary people were willing to obey given the right situation (authority figure and gradual commitment – increments of 15 volts). In support of these findings many further studies were carried out and showed this was not a one-off phenomena. Most recently Russell (2011) carried out a close replica of the original study and found results had not changed over time, or across gender, showing that Milligram's study was reliable and his results in laboratory conditions were valid.

The study was criticised for being artificial, therefore ecologically invalid. So Milgram took the study to a run-down office building. Though the obedience declined, there were still significant obedience levels. Some said the participants realised they weren't giving real electric shocks, but recorded reactions of the participants clearly show real distress in some participants. This study was also highly criticised for its lack of ethical care of the participants.

Some studies (Reicher & Haslam, 2011; Russell, 2011) argue that Milgram's study, though ground breaking and useful, took the focus from the variation in obedience and why it really happens. Reicher & Haslam argue for it to be explained via Social identity theory, which pivots on who the person identifies most closely with. In the Milgram study, the participant identifies most closely with the researcher and takes orders from him more readily.

See also:
Research: ethics.

References

ADORNO, T. W. et al (1950) The Authoritarian Personality. New York: Harper and Row.

KOHLBERG, L. (1973) The Claim to Moral Adequacy of a Highest Stage of Moral Judgment. *Journal of Philosophy*. 70 (18). pp.630–46.

MILGRAM, S. (1963) Behavioral Study of Obedience. *Journal of Abnormal and Social Psychology*. 67 (4). pp.371–8.

REICHER, S. & HASLAM, S. A. (2011) After Shock? Towards a Social Identity Explanation of Milgram's 'Obedience Studies'. *British Journal of Social Psychology*. 50. pp.163–9.

RUSSELL, N. J. C. (2011) Milgram's Obedience to Authority Experiments: Origins and Early Evolution. *British Journal of Social Psychology*. 50. pp.140–62.

ROTTER, J. B. (1966) Generalized Expectancies of Internal versus External Control of Reinforcements. *Psychological Monographs*. 80 (609).

ZIMBARDO, P. (2007) *The Lucifer Effect*. New York: The Random House.

OBEs and NDEs

Anomalistic psychologists focus on experiences that are considered to be 'out of the ordinary'. This concept considers out-of-body experiences (OBE) and near-death experiences (NDE).

An OBE has been described as feeling separate from your own body so that you can look down on what is happening. An NDE happens when the person is thought to be close to death, or they are clinically dead for a short while.

Description of OBE and NDE

According to Blackmore (1982), an OBE is 'an experience in which a person seems to perceive the world from a location outside the physical body.' It often happens when a person is under extraordinary stress. Around 20% of the world population has had an OBE which occur across cultures, gender, age and educational levels.

An NDE is a more extreme experience, which in fact often incorporates an OBE. For example, a man who was clinically dead for a short while during a surgical procedure, claimed he could hear the conversation the surgical team were having during his crisis. He was able to accurately give specific details of the conversation, which he should have known nothing about. He was also able to describe what he could see of the operation when he was out of his body.

Some or all of the following characteristics may be included in an NDE:

➤ Viewing own body, as it is being resuscitated.

➤ Vivid and dramatic accounts of feeling near death, though you don't necessarily have to be near death in reality to have one of these

➤ A feeling of contentment and moving down a tunnel into the light, along with sightings of long dead loved ones, spirits and even religious figures, such as God

➤ A utopian environment, where everything is idyllic and beautiful and a feeling of getting to a point where they would either die or return to their body.

Whatever the experience, most people who have experienced NDE and OBE to some extent report life changing feelings, with greater love for mankind, less fear of the unknown, greater spirituality and a need to do good.

Evaluation of OBE and NDE

The explanations for both OBE and NDE fall into two areas: paranormal theories and scientific psychological theories.

The paranormal theories are:

1. The physical (body) and the non-physical (mind) can indeed separate.

2. The second explanation suggests information is received via extra-sensory perception, therefore giving the perception that the mind has left the body. However, this simply explains one anomalistic experience with another.

3. Transcendental hypothesis suggests an NDE is exactly what it appears to be, where the person does leave their physical body. The main problem with this theory is that it is not falsifiable, and therefore not scientific.

Some experts believe an overall weakness of paranormal theories is that the information could have been received in some other way.

The scientific psychological theories are:

1. Blackmore's theory (see Research, below) that a person's reality is sometimes no more than imagination and memories, rather than a result of actual sensory input.

2. A neuro-scientific theory of NDE, which is more valued by scientists is the 'dying brain hypothesis', where there is abnormal activity in the brain.

The main advantage of a scientific theory is that it produces a testable hypothesis. However. just because something is testable does not necessarily make it true. And conversely, just because something is not testable, does not make it untrue.

Research: OBE

According to Blackmore (1987), people who have OBE experiences generally view the experience as an onlooker, rather than being part of the action (observer perspective). She also theorised that observer perspective was the most common view in dreams and imagination, but the least common when a person is recalling a real life event. Blakemore's view was that an OBE was, in essence, nothing more than fantasy. The use of observer perspective in OBE recall would support this idea.

In a series of three studies, Blackmore found that people who had OBE experiences were indeed more likely to use observer perspective for dream recall, but not for real-life events. They were also better able to switch perspectives, which she felt offered support for her model, that OBE people would be able to switch perspectives quite easily compared to non-OBE people. The OBE people were also seen to have better spatial imagery (Cook & Irwin 1983) and superior dream control skills (Blakemore 1986).

As a result of research, it has been found that OBEs can in fact be induced by deliberately disrupting various sources of sensory information input and not allowing them to interact in the correct way; this is termed 'bottom-up'. Ehrsson (2007) did this bottom-up process, using virtual reality technology, where participants were given a view of their back from about two metres away. They then used a rod to touch the participant's chest, out of view, which gave a tactile illusion, so that the participants felt they were actually out of their own bodies. While this does appear to stimulate an OBE, it does not provide evidence for or against OBEs; it just means the feeling of being out of one's body can be simulated.

Case study: OBEs

Generally, OBEs happen when there is a crisis of some sort, which was the case with Olivia. After a long and difficult labour, she gave birth to a disabled child. The disability came as a shock, as there had been no prior warning.

After the birth was over, time seemed to stand still, Olivia felt she was floating above her body and was able to see the midwife in the corner looking worried and her husband holding the baby and him crying. She felt she had a choice of whether to return and face the reality, or to stay out of reality. She chose to face whatever would come.

It felt like the OBE had lasted a long time, but in fact, it was probably just seconds. As Olivia had been given a pain-killing injection, perhaps this was just a chemical reaction, but to Olivia it felt real.

References

BLACKMORE, S. J. (1982) *Beyond the Body: An Investigation of Out-of-the-Body Experience*. London: Paladin, 1.

BLACKMORE, S. J. (1987) Where Am I? Perspectives in Imagery, and the Out-of-Body Experience. *Journal of Mental Imagery*. 11. pp.53–66.

COOK, A. M. & IRWIN, H. J. (1983) Visuospatial Skills and the Out-of-Body Experience. *Journal of Parapsychology*. 47. pp.23–35.

EHRSSON, H. H. (2007) The Experimental Induction of Out-of-Body Experiences. *Science*. 317. p.1048.

Research: data types

It is important to know what type of data is produced from research, as it influences analysis decisions, such as what measure of central tendency to use (mean, median or mode) and what type of inferential test will need to be carried out to find out if results are significant or not. When the data produced is numerical, it generally produces the following types of data: nominal, ordinal, interval or ratio.

Descriptive and inferential statistics

Descriptive statistics are used to condense a large amount of information into a useable form. This will allow interpretation of what sets of numbers mean in an efficient and clear way. The descriptive statistics will therefore be a set of averages or norms of the data being analysed. There are two types of measurement in descriptive statistics: measures of central tendency (central figure, such as; mean, median and mode) and measure of dispersion (spread of data, such as standard deviation, distribution and range).

Inferential statistics is the process of analysing the data to draw conclusions about from the data generated from studies. The type of data will be one of the factors that determine which test should be used in the analysis. For example, if data is nominal, the chi-squared test is a suitable inferential test (i.e. a test that looks for significance) when looking for a difference in conditions. The whole point of an inferential test is to see if the results are significant, or due to chance.

Levels of measurement

There are four levels of measurement that differ in precision and sensitivity: nominal, ordinal, interval and ratio.

Nominal

Nominal data consist of numbers of participants falling into different, mutually exclusive categories, e.g. fat, thin; men, women. The measure of central tendency used here would be mode.

If a researcher wanted to group people according to their eating preferences, such as meat-eaters, vegetarians, vegans and fruitarians, this would be an example of nominal data.

1   2

Ordinal

In ordinal scales, the data can be ordered from largest to smallest, or first to last, as in finishing positions in a competition. The measures of central tendency used would be median or mode.

Interval

Interval scales differ from ordinal because the units of measurement are fixed throughout the range. For example, in intelligence testing the distance between 100 and 110 is equal to the distance between 100 and 90. With ordinal scales of measurement, the distance is variable; the distance between 1st and 2nd is not necessarily the same as the distance between 2nd and 3rd.

Sometimes it may be unclear whether data are ordinal or interval; if in doubt, ordinal should be used for the purpose of analysis.

Ratio

Ratio data have the same characteristics as interval data, but they have a meaningful zero point. For example, time measurements provide ratio data because zero time is meaningful, i.e. 10 seconds is twice as long as 5 seconds. Similarities between interval and ratio data are so close that they are sometimes joined together as interval/ratio data. The measures of central tendency that can be used are: mean and median.

Research: Celec et al (2002)

Celec et al (2002) investigated whether testosterone levels in young women had an effect on their spatial ability over the course of their menstrual cycle. Participants provided daily saliva samples to assess testosterone levels. The findings showed that testosterone peaked just before ovulation. It also showed that when the testosterone levels were at their highest, the women performed better on spatial tasks. This can be classed as interval/ratio data.

References

CELEC, P. et al (2002) The Circalunar Cycle of Salivary Testosterone and the Visual-Spatial Performance. *Bratislavske Lekavske Listy.* 103. pp.59–69.

COOLICAN, H. (2004) *Introduction to Research Methods and Statistics in Psychology.* London: Hodder & Stoughton.

Research: design

In psychological research the design refers simply to how participants take part in the study. Whenever researchers set up a study, they need to consider which design is most appropriate, depending on the nature or circumstances of the study or what the study is aiming to investigate.

Experimental research design

In experimental studies the researcher is generally looking for a difference between two or more groups, called conditions. The researcher has to decide how they are going to use their participants in the different conditions.

There are three main types of design: repeated measures, matched pairs and independent measures. There are advantages and disadvantages to each type of design.

Repeated measures

One option is to have all groups take part in all conditions (repeated measures, so called because participants repeat the test – see research example below). A variation of this design is where participants perform the *same* task at different time points, e.g. aged 16 and then aged 18.

An advantage of repeated measures is that it needs fewer people and individual differences between participants are not an issue (as with independent measures). A disadvantage is that there may be order effects (e.g. boredom or fatigue resulting from the order in which the tasks are performed) and increased possibility of demand characteristics (where participants are aware of the research situation which affects how they perform). Also, the potential uses for this kind of research design are limited.

Research example
Ramponi *et al.* (2004), investigating age differences in levels of processing, used a repeated measures design: the two age groups took part in all levels of processing. This was also independent measures design, as participants could only be in the older or younger group.

See also:
Memory: levels
of processing.

Matched pairs and independent measures

It may be important that participants take part in separate conditions. In this case there are two options:

➤ **Matched pairs design** – each group of participants is carefully matched for particular characteristics, such as age or IQ. The benefit of this is that there will be no order effects and individual differences will be minimised. The drawbacks are that there will have to be a larger number of people available and it is difficult to achieve complete matches. In addition, this design is more time-consuming for the researcher than the other types of design.

➤ **Independent measure design** – different participants are used in separate conditions, but no characteristics are matched. This stops the order effects of repeated measures design, but does not require as many participants as matched pairs design. However, there is room for error resulting from individual differences.

Research example
In a study into how stress affects the immune system, Kiecolt-Glaser et al (1995) compared home carers (high-stress group) and non-carers (low-stress group). They needed to put groups in separate conditions. To eliminate many individual differences between the two, they chose a matched pairs design, matching participants for example by gender and age.

Case study: research design in practice

If a teacher wants to test whether girls or boys are better at mathematics, the design has to be either independent measures or matched pairs design, as participants can only be in a male or female group. As the investigation concerns academic ability, it would be appropriate to match the girls and boys for IQ level. If the students are matched, then it becomes a matched pairs design.

References

KIECOLT-GLASER, et al (1995) Slowing of Wound Healing by Psychological stress. *The Lancet.* 346. pp.1194–6.

RAMPONI, C. et al Levels of Processing and Age Affect Involuntary Conceptual Priming of Weak But Not Strong Associates. *Experimental Psychology.* 51. pp.159–64.

Research: ethics

In psychology, ethics are fundamental moral principles that respect the rights and feelings of those taking part in research, as well as their physical and emotional well-being. Ethical issues arise in research where there is a conflict between the rights and dignity of participants and the goals and outcomes of research. As some psychologists research into non-humans, there is a separate set of guidelines to cover this area.

Codes of ethics

In response to ethical issues, codes of ethics are developed: sets of moral guidelines and responsibilities that psychologists and researchers into psychological phenomena should follow. Codes of ethics are there to protect the rights of the participant and try to make sure they come to no lasting harm from their participation in studies. The code of ethics set out by such recognised bodies as the BPS (British Psychological Society) not only protect participants, both human and non-human, but also the researchers. Codes of ethics are not limited to research, but also extend to how psychologists conduct themselves.

Enforcing the guidelines
In the UK, the BPS has the power to impose penalties on any members who infringe their ethical code, including expulsion from the Society. However, as professional psychologists are not obliged to join the BPS, this sanction is not as powerful as in, say, the medical profession, where doctors who are struck off may not practise medicine.

Ethical principles

The BPS code of conduct is based on four ethical principles, which set out the 'main domains of responsibility within which ethical issues are considered' (BPS, 2009).

Respect

This means treating everyone involved in research with 'dignity and worth' and avoiding 'unfair or prejudiced practice', including such issues as: anonymity, privacy, deception, confidentiality, and asking permission to record responses in a variety of ways, such as media recordings. Participants need to be given all facts prior to consenting to take part in a study and be aware of their right to withdraw without prejudice.

Competence

All psychologists need to work competently at a level appropriate to their situation, skills and experience. This means being aware of their own and other's limits in the working party, along with full awareness of all legal and moral guidelines to be adhered to. These factors are about the psychologist's responsibility to safeguard both the public and the profession of psychology. Competence also includes avoiding harm to participants and preventing abuse or misuse, thus preventing misconduct, which would bring the profession into disrepute. The psychologist also has to be aware of colleagues' conduct and of potential risks to themselves.

Responsibility

Psychologists have a duty to protect participants in research. This means protecting their psychological and physical well-being and adhering to the BPS guidelines. If any harm happens inadvertently, researchers need to ensure they take measures to deal with this, including debriefing and support during and post research.

Integrity

Psychologists are expected to conduct themselves with integrity. This means being honest, accurate and clear to all people in all matters. It also requires psychologists to act professionally and not abuse any position within the profession – for example, psychologists should not commit scientific fraud (e.g. by tampering with results of a study in order to get it published).

Research that raises ethical issues

Many well-known studies from the past have proved controversial because they appear to violate ethical principles, such as Milgram's obedience study. These studies took place before a code of ethics was established. However, one beneficial result of these studies was they got psychologists discussing the need for ethical guidelines, which today are an integral part of the profession. One such study is that of Zimbardo et al (1973), which was created to Investigate conformity to social role, a form of social influence.

See also:
Conformity;
Obedience.

Zimbardo et al's 'Stanford prison experiment' (1973)
After this study, Zimbardo suggested that people who are given a particular role to perform will adhere to that in various degrees of commitment. People who conform to the role completely will submerge themselves so completely, they will become deindividuated. In Zimbardo et al's simulated prison experiment there were instances of deception – the participants selected as 'prisoners' were not told in advance that they would be arrested very publicly by real police. Zimbardo allowed participants to undergo physical and psychological distress without intervening and also stopped participants withdrawing. Due to the amount of harm being caused to participants, the study was finally stopped early, but this was not before several participants had severe psychological reactions to the situation. However, like Milgram before him, who also crossed the boundaries of what was acceptable, Zimbardo gave extensive debriefing after the study, which is one way in which a psychologists can try and right the wrongs of what happened during the procedure of a study.

Ethics in practice

Today, if a researcher wants to carry out a study, they have to write a proposal to be approved by an ethics committee. One of the components on that proposal is explaining how they meet ethical guidelines. If for any reason they cannot meet all guidelines, they will have to justify why not. For example, justification may include the claim that if participants understood the full nature of the study, they might not act naturally.

When participants take part in a study, they should be aware of their rights from the start. These should be set out in 'informed consent forms'. During and after the study, the researcher has to ensure they follow the ethical guidelines and be mindful to protect participants.

Research using non-humans

As with humans, past research with non-humans triggered concerns for their welfare, particularly after the Harlow's monkey experiment (1958), where monkeys were taken away from their mothers at birth and were deprived of any contact with other monkeys. Instead they were left to live in small units with inanimate dummies symbolising surrogate mothers.

At that time there were no ethical guidelines for researchers to abide by. In response to these concerns, Russell and Burch (1959) created 'The principles of humane experimental techniques', summarised as the three Rs:

➤ Refine – experimental procedures to minimise suffering.

➤ Reduce – the number of animals used to the bare minimum required.

➤ Replace – the use of animals with other means whenever possible.

A fund was also set up – the Lord Dowding Fund for Humane Research. This has helped produce research using MRIs and PET scans in humans, along with computer simulations to reduce the need to use non-humans.

Ethical guidelines

More recently, the British Psychological Society (BPS) issued ethical guidelines that psychological researchers should adhere to. It recently revised its advice on working with animals (2012). These guidelines stress the following points:

➤ It is essential to comply with legislation.

➤ The species used for research should be suitable.

➤ Before embarking on research, there needs to be thorough knowledge of previous research, so animals are not put through unnecessary suffering.

➤ The number of animals used to be kept to a minimum.

➤ Animals must be sourced from legitimate suppliers who are known to treat their livestock well.

References

BPS (BRITISH PSYCHOLOGICAL SOCIETY) (2009) *Code of Ethics and Conduct Guidance*. Leicester: The Ethics Committee of the BPS.

BPS (BRITISH PSYCHOLOGICAL SOCIETY) (2012) *Guidelines for Psychologists Working with Animals*. Leicester: The Research Board of the BPS.

HARLOW, H. (1958) The Nature of Love. *American Psychologist*. 13. pp.673–85.

MILGRAM, S. (1963) Behavioural Study of Obedience. *Journal of Abnormal and Social Psychology*. 67. pp.391–8.

RUSSELL, W. M. S. & BURCH, R. L. (1959) *The Principles of Humane Experimental Technique*. London: Methuen.

Research: methods

Research in psychology is essential for providing evidence for theories. The method chosen by a researcher for investigating a phenomenon is influenced by the approach they working from, as some approaches value quantitative methods more than qualitative and vice versa.

Investigative methods in psychology

Mainstream psychology has a preference for quantitative methods, as they provide empirical evidence and allow for making broad-ranging assumptions about likely behaviour in the population (nomothetic). Qualitative methods, however, provide unique complex information on how the whole person thinks, feels and behaves (idiographic).

Methods favoured by different approaches
Different psychological approaches favour different methods of investigation:

➤ Biological, behavioural and cognitive approaches generally favour quantitative methods more than qualitative.

➤ The psychodynamic approach was originally built on case studies (qualitative).

➤ The humanist approach is opposed to nomothetic methods (quantitative) in its basic principles and so favours idiographic methods (qualitative).

Quantitative methods

Quantitative methods provide data in numerical form (numbers). They are used when researchers want to measures variables and look for differences between groups. They are suited to testing emergent theories and hypotheses.

Examples of quantitative methods are experiments, structured questionnaires and observations.

Advantages

➤ Quantitative methods used to seek empirical support for theories and enable prediction of future behaviour.

➤ Studies with this method have a degree of control, are replicable and use the hypothetico-deductive method (cross ref to science and pseudo science)

See also:
Science and
pseudo-science.

Disadvantages

➤ Quantitative methods can be argued to be reductionist, as they usually involve a narrow contrived snapshot of behaviour.

➤ There is more likelihood of participant and investigator bias.

➤ There is more likely to be a lack of mundane realism and ecological validity, particularly in lab experiments.

➤ The ethical issue of deception is more likely to be a problem, as deception is often needed to try and ensure true behaviour.

See also:
Research:
reliability &
validity.

Types of experiment

Laboratory experiments

These are experiments that are carried out in a controlled environment. They have the highest degree of experimental validity (internal validity) because there is less chance of extraneous variables affecting the dependent variable (DV). In this type of experiment, the researcher will manipulate the independent variable (IV) and will be able to establish cause and effect if there is a difference in the experimental group/s compared to the control group.

Field experiments
Field experiments are carried out in a more natural environment, therefore have less control than a lab experiment, and so lower internal validity, but have a higher ecological validity. The IV is manipulated by the researcher, and again cause and effect can be established.

Natural experiments
In natural experiments there is an IV and DV, but the IV happens naturally, as it is impossible or unethical to manipulate the IV. There is a problem with inferring a causal relationship, as the IV is not directly manipulated. This method does allow psychologists to study what happens in the 'real' world, however. This means it has high mundane realism and ecological validity.

Quasi-experiment
The quasi-experiment (Cook & Campbell 1979) is sometimes referred to as 'not quite an experiment', as it is missing some vital elements, such as not having experimental control in manipulating the IV and/or random allocation of the participants to conditions. A natural experiment is a type of quasi experiment.

The quasi-experiment was developed to help give credit to studies outside the laboratory and expand psychology beyond the mentality that lab experiments were superior to all other forms of investigation.

Qualitative methods

Qualitative methods are not concerned with numbers, but with descriptive data. They often involve observing people and finding out about them through how they express themselves and what they are saying The primary concern is with attitudes, feelings and beliefs from individual experience. They are suited to exploring new areas of behaviour and developing new theories.

Examples of qualitative methods are: case studies, content analysis, diaries, semi-structured and unstructured questionnaires and interviews, and natural observations.

Advantages

➤ Qualitative methods offer greater mundane realism (real-world meaning).

➤ They look at the phenomenon as a whole, so all aspects are taken into account.

➤ There is subjectivity, and researchers will sometimes collaborate with participants as equal partners to gain a more honest account of phenomena.

➤ The inductive method is used, meaning research works from the bottom up, i.e. investigation will start from an observation, which will lead to detection of patterns, which will lead to development of theories from the data obtained.

Disadvantages

➤ Most of the data is not replicable; findings are therefore lacking in internal validity and cannot be falsified.

➤ Data cannot be readily generalised to a larger population, as this type of method usually only uses a limited population.

Qualitative research in practice

Questionnaires

The qualitative method of carrying out a questionnaire differs from the quantitative in several ways.

➤ When putting together the questionnaire, there will be a research question, rather than a hypothesis as in quantitative research. This is to avoid any possible bias on the researcher's part. A hypothesis could also be seen to restrict the possibilities of discovering new theories.

➤ Participant numbers will be smaller than in quantitative method, where a large volume of participants is often preferred.

➤ The sampling method is more likely to be 'purposive sampling', where participants are chosen for their appropriateness for the study focus.

Interviews and observations
When compiling results from interviews and observations, researchers using quantitative methods are interested in gathering and analysing numerical data. However, researchers using qualitative methods will record not only the interview or observation, but also peripheral activity such as paralinguistics (laughter, pauses, facial expressions) of the participant. They may also record the researcher's own thoughts and feelings in order to establish whether there was any bias present.

Research: natural experiment (Charlton et al)

An interesting example of a natural experiment was carried out by Charlton et al (2002). They used a unique opportunity that arose to test children in several categories, such as pro- and antisocial behaviour before and after the introduction of television to the South Atlantic island of St Helena in 1995. It was a natural experiment because the IV (the introduction of television) was not controlled by the psychologists, but instead was a naturally occurring event. A combination of quantitative and qualitative data were collected:

➤ Quantitative data were compiled from observations that were specifically looking at incidence of aggressive play. Cameras recorded the children in the classroom and playground for aggressive play. There were also questionnaires for parents and teachers.

➤ Qualitative methods included content analysis of the television viewed and reports from the teachers and parents.

Combining quantitative and qualitative

In practice, it is often not a case of choosing quantitative or qualitative methods, as both types of methods can be used together in research studies. Examples of this include Milgram's experiment into obedience (1963) and Zimbardo et al.'s (1973) 'Stanford prison experiment' on conformity. Both studies used the quantitative method of laboratory experiment, but when collating data, the researchers not only calculated the percentages of obedience and conformity, but they also included comments from the participants.

References

CHARLTON, T., HANNAN, A. & GUNTER, B. (eds.) (2002) *Broadcast TV Effects in a Remote Community* (Mahaw): New Jersey: Lawrence Erlbaum Associates.

COOK, T. D. & CAMPBELL, D. T. (1979) *Quasi-experimentation: Design and Analysis Issues for Field Settings.* Chicago: Rand McNally.

COOLICAN, H. (1999) *Research Methods and Statistics in Psychology.* 3rd Ed. London: Hodder & Stoughton.

MILGRAM, S. (1963). Behavioral Study of Obedience. *Journal of Abnormal and Social Psychology.* 67. pp.371–8.

ZIMBARDO, P. G. et al (1973) 'Pirandellian prison: the mind is a formidable jailor', *New York Times Magazine*, 8 April, pp.38–60.

Research: reliability & validity

Reliability is the extent to which a test, measurement or classification system produces the same scientific observation each time it is applied, i.e. whether the study is replicable.

Validity is the extent to which a research method does actually measure what it sets out to measure. There are various types of validity, including internal and external validity.

Internal and external reliability

A distinction can be made between internal and external reliability. Internal reliability involves making sure the measurement is consistent *within the method*. For example, in a questionnaire, it means checking that all questions are measuring the same thing. In an IQ test, all questions should be equal in difficulty throughout the test.

External reliability is about whether or not the method of measurement generates consistent results each time it is used. For example, if an IQ test is carried out a month apart with the same person, it should produce the same, or a very similar, result. If it doesn't, external reliability is low.

Checking reliability

Split-half method
This test can check internal reliability. If doing this test, the researcher will split the test and mark it as test (a) and test (b). The participant then takes both parts as if they were two tests, and the results are compared, e.g. to see whether an IQ test has a consistent level of difficulty in both parts. The results of each test will be compared by correlation; if similar or the same results, the test is internally reliable.

The test–retest method

This is used to check external reliability. Here, the same test is used with the same participant with a suitable time gap between tests and the results are then compared, e.g. the same IQ test could be taken twice, with a two-week time gap in between tests and the results compared for similarity. The time gap between tests has to be long enough to ensure the test cannot be remembered by the participant, as this would cause a problem with internal validity.

Inter-rater reliability test

This is used when there are a number of researchers carrying out the same procedure, such as an observation. It works by having two or more observers watch the same behaviour, e.g. from a filmed observation, and then comparing all the observers' ratings to check they are all similar.

Research: Rosenhan (1973)

The construction and revising of the DSM (Diagnostic and Statistical Manual of Mental Disorder) since its introduction has been mainly due to issues of reliability and validity. It is important for a diagnosis to be correct, as error could lead to a series of consequences for the patient.

In a famous study by Rosenhan (1973), he tested how safe the diagnosis of insanity was across 12 different psychiatric hospitals in the USA. The hospitals varied in size, prestige and facilities. Rosenhan used three women and five men, as well as himself. None of the volunteers had a history of mental illness. They ranged from a housewife to professional people. One male was in his 20s, the others more mature. The only thing they faked was a report of hearing voices, because of which they were admitted to psychiatric wards, where they proceeded to act normally. The psychiatrist diagnosed one with schizophrenia, and most of the others were diagnosed as being in remission from schizophrenia. The only people aware they were sane were many of the genuine patients, who at times protested this loudly. The volunteers were patients for an average of 19 days. When the psychiatric hospitals were made aware of these findings, one of them challenged Rosenhan to send more pseudo-patients to them and they would be able to spot them. In one weekend, the hospital in question had nearly 200 new patients and ruled that 41 of them were pseudo-patients and there was suspicion that several others were too. Yet, Rosenhan never sent any pseudo-patients. This study highlighted the inadequacy of the DSM-III in the diagnosis of psychotic disorder. It was subsequently revised.

Internal validity

Internal validity is concerned with whether the measurements are really as a result of what was tested, or whether there was there interference from an extraneous variable (EV) and/or  a confounding variable (CV). For example, if carrying out an experiment, is any change in the dependent variable (DV) a result of the independent variable (IV – the variable that is being manipulated), or is it really a measurement of an EV or CV?

External validity

External validity concerns itself with whether the results can be generalised to a wider population. In other words, are the results limited to a particular context or would the same results be found in any environment – another place, using other people or at another point in time?

➤ **Ecological validity** refers to the environment in which a study takes place. For example, if the results were generated in a laboratory experiment, would people still have acted the same way in a natural environment? If not, then there is a lack of ecological validity.

➤ **Population validity** concerns the sample group of people used in a study and whether it is representative of the target population as a whole. For example, if a study looks at how early attachment affects the socialisation of teenage boys and the researcher only uses a sample of boys with behavioural problems, it would not be valid to generalise findings to the larger target population of all teenage boys.

➤ **Historical validity** tests whether results from a study in the past can be related to the present or indeed the future. Do the results stand the test of time or do they just present a snapshot of a particular period?

Extraneous and confounding variables

Internal validity concerns itself with avoiding possible extraneous and confounding variables. These terms are often confused, but an extraneous variable is a general term for unwanted effects on the dependent variable. A confounding variable is more specific, as it is an extraneous variable that systematically varies with the independent variable. Extraneous variables can take different forms, often depending on the type of method and design.

Participant effects

➤ The Hawthorne effect – where a person acts differently because they know they are being observed.

➤ Demand characteristics – where the person may try to second-guess the researcher and act the way they think they are supposed to act, whether to help or hinder. This will in turn cause the participant to act unnaturally, making the result unsafe to generalise to other populations.

➤ Social desirability bias – where the participant wants to look good and acts accordingly: for example, if there is a questionnaire about parental attachment to their children, they may answer questions that makes them look like a good parent, rather than tell the truth.

Investigator effects

➤ Experimenter or investigator bias (not every investigation is an experiment) – where the researcher's behaviour affects the results. Often this happens indirectly, such as in standardised instruction; the researcher may want a particular outcome and so phrases the instructions to help it happen.

➤ Operationalising variables – when variables that are not measurable, such as romantic love, are given measurable elements, such as measures of intimacy between two people. Depending on the investigator's ideas of romantic love, these measures may be prone to bias.

➤ Stereotyping or prejudice – the way a researcher relates to participants may affect responses without the researcher being aware of it, e.g. a researcher may have certain stereotypes about gender roles so that he acts differently towards male and female participants.

Environmental effects

➤ Level of noise could have an impact on concentration, or may irritate, causing the participant to respond to the noise, rather that the IV.

➤ Temperature – a very hot or cold room can affect participants' concentration and/or mood.

➤ Level of light – can also affect concentration and mood.

➤ Configuration of a room – how the room is set-up.

Checking internal validity

Aspects of internal validity that can be checked are:

➤ Face validity – this is a simple subjective assessment of whether the test appears to measure what it aims to. It is a crude measure and it is difficult to judge whether or not such that things as social desirability and demand characteristics occurred to render the test invalid.

➤ Concurrent validity – this is where a newly designed self-report, such as a questionnaire, is compared with a previously validated one on the same topic. The participants would be given both questionnaires in one sitting and the results compared for similarity.

➤ Predictive validity – is about whether a test score is really an indicator of future performance or not. For example, if a person achieves a high score on an IQ score, they could be expected to perform well in an exam or other measure of their academic intelligence. If predictive and actual performance are similar, a test can be said to be valid.

➤ Construct validity – is about examining whether measurement tools actually measure the construct being investigated, e.g. a questionnaire asking about how childhood attachment affected later romantic relationships should have questions relevant to theory in that area, such as attachment theory.

References

COOLICAN, H. (1999) Research Methods and Statistics in Psychology. 3rd Ed. London: Hodder & Stoughton.

ROSENHAN, D. L. (1973) On Being Sane in Insane Places. Science. 179 (4070). pp.250–8.

Science & pseudo-science

Science is a particular way of looking at the world that emphasises objectivity, falsifiability and replicability. Generally, it formulates a hypothesis prior to carrying out a study. Pseudo-science is thought by some to be false science. Webster's Dictionary defines it as relying on 'deceptive or fallacious arguments called sophisms'. It is considered to be a pathway of research that believes itself to be scientific, but really is not. Therefore the results cannot be considered any more than anecdotal.

Principles of science

In order to be scientific, something has to be testable, repeatable, falsifiable (able to be proved false) and open to change, to allow for the given theory to evolve. It also has to stand up to criticism and be able to respond to unresolved questions by means of further research. The main methodological approach of science is use of the hypothetico-deductive method, whereby a hypothesis (a prediction of what may happen) is given and research is then carried out to investigate whether or not it is true.

Pseudo-science, however, lacks some or all of the main principles of science.

See also:
Anomalistic psychology.

Features of pseudo-science

Randi (2001) identified six main features of pseudo-science, in contrast to science:

➤ It does not make any sense and is therefore devoid of logic.

➤ It is inconsistent – supposedly related phenomena do not have common ground.

➤ It does not stay within accepted scientific principles, e.g. often relying on anecdotal and testimonial evidence.

➤ It is often based on the word of one leader or an accepted text with no foundation.

➤ It is unchanging and therefore does not respond to new findings.

As there is no quantifiable evidence, it cannot be used to predict future events or behaviour (a feature of science).

Dutch (2006) suggests that pseudo-science exists to validate a pre-assumed truth. Dutch also identifies various types of pseudo-science, such as mystical pseudo-science used to explain paranormal experiences, or tabloid pseudo-science that exists to entertain and intrigue, such as theories surrounding the Loch Ness Monster.

Comparing science and pseudo-science

The table above contrasts the main features of science and pseudo-science.

Science	Pseudo-science
Research findings are subjected to peer review.	Results are communicated directly to the public, thus avoiding peer scrutiny.
The advancement of humankind generally drives research.	Self-justification or self-promotion are often the basis for research.
A hypothesis is formulated, and data then gathered and analysed.	A hypothesis is often formulated in retrospect in order to support data gathered.
Methodological pluralism is often used to validate scientific analysis, i.e. hypothesis is thoroughly tested and if necessary can be falsified.	Myths, anecdotes and personal testimonies are used to support research findings.
Burden of supplying evidence is on those making any claim.	Burden of supplying evidence is placed on those sceptical of the claim.
Focus is on testing only what actually happens.	Focus is often on testing what might happen, using outdated unsupported theories.
There is continual updating based on solid research methods.	Often ignores conventional science and disagreement.

The table above contrasts the main features of science and pseudo-science.

However, there are similarities between the two:

➤ They both have a research question, formulate a hypothesis, investigate it and publish the findings (though science formulates an idea to test and pseudo-science tests an already established idea to prove it).

➤ Both select their chosen areas of study and can sometimes be guilty of letting a personal need for gain from their research get in the way of the truth.

➤ They both generate data in much the same way and they can both use a variety of different methods.

Scientific fraud

Scientific fraud is a very real issue in psychology and anomalistic psychology is considered particularly prone to it. An example of such a case was of the Cottingly Fairies, where two sisters decided to have a bit of fun and place cut-out paper fairies in front of a camera then say the fairies were real. This happened in 1917 and, although their father saw it as a prank, their mother showed the pictures to an occult conference. Sir Arthur Conan Doyle publicly supported the idea that the fairies were real. In 1966 the sisters finally admitted it had been a hoax. Interest in the hoax had mostly continued because people wanted to believe in the fairies.

Scientific fraud can also be a problem with mainstream psychology. One such case was Sir Cyril Burt's correlation study of MZ twins reared apart and their IQ scores. His findings reported a very significant +0.771 correlation, which was near to a perfect match to the findings of his pilot study. The British Psychological Society, of which he had been President, found him guilty of fraud.

However, despite such cases, the suspicion of fraud is much more common with anomalistic psychology, mainly due to the pseudo-scientific methods sometimes employed. It is worth emphasising that such methods are generally employed by non-psychologists and that any psychologists involved have worked hard to make the methods rigorous.

See also: OBEs and NDEs.

References

DUTCH, S. (2006) *Science and Pseudoscience*. Madison, WI: University of Wisconsin Press.

RADNER, D. & Radner, M. (1982) *Science and Unreason*. Belmont, CA: Wadsworth.

RANDI, J. (2001) *Science and Pseudoscience*. Fort Lauderdale, FL: The James Randi Educational Foundation.

Sleeping: explanations

There are three main approaches that seek to explain the functions of sleep, i.e. why and if people and animals need to enter this state of inactivity and dormancy. The explanations are evolutionary theory (sometimes referred to as ecological), restoration theory and brain plasticity.

Evolutionary explanation (ecological)

The evolutionary theory suggests that sleep is an adaptive behaviour to aid survival and is therefore essential to all animal and human life.

Hibernation theory (Webb 1974)

Hibernation theory states that humans and other warm-blooded animals have high metabolic rates and so expend lots of energy on maintaining a constant body temperature. Sleep serves the purpose of enforced inactivity and so preserves energy. Sleep is therefore thought to be relative to metabolic rate and foraging requirements (e.g. whether herbivore or carnivore). For example:

➤ Herbivores such as cows have to spend many hours foraging due to the low nutrition in their diet, so have less time sleeping.

➤ Carnivores have highly nutritious diets and so have more time to sleep and thereby conserve energy.

Predator avoidance (Meddis 1975)

This theory suggests that if an animal is primarily a predator, then they can afford to sleep for long periods as they are not in danger of attack. For prey animals, however, sleep is a time of enforced inactivity, where they can keep out of harm's way from their predators at times of most danger. For most species that is during night time hours, but for nocturnal creatures, it can be during daylight.

Evaluation of evolutionary explanations

On one level the evolutionary explanations seem feasible, providing an explanation for why sleep is necessary and for the variation in amount of sleep for different species. However, this explanation has been criticised on several grounds:

➤ It is difficult to test evolutionary explanations and hence find substantiated evidence for them. Evolutionary theory by its very nature is generally retrospective (looks backward) and fits into a hypothesis, rather than being hypothetico-deductive.

See also:
Science and
pseudo-science.

➤ Predator avoidance seems an unlikely explanation, as it would be safer to be alert and still, rather than unconscious and unable to flee or defend self.

➤ This theory also begs the question: why hasn't sleep disappeared (i.e. been evolved out), when it would be more beneficial for an animal *not* to sleep? Carlson (1994) observed that Indus dolphins living in the muddy waters of Pakistan have become blind because eyesight is unnecessary. Instead they have an exceptional sonar system that enables them to navigate the waters, forage for food and find mates. These mammals, which swim constantly, have not had their sleep eliminated – instead they sleep in 4–60 seconds intervals over a 7-hour period. The fact sleep still exists, suggests there is another reason for it, than purely predator avoidance or energy conservation.

Restoration theories

Restoration theory assumes that sleep restores our brain and body's energy and faculties, through a process of reconfiguration in the brain and a period of rest for the body.

Oswald's restoration model (1980)

Oswald (1980) suggested that the energy expended during waking hours was recouped during sleep. Rapid eye movement (REM) sleep – the deepest level of sleep – was thought to be important for brain growth and repair, with slow-wave sleep (SWS) being important for bodily growth and repair.

Horne's core/optional sleep model (1988)

Horne extended Oswald's ideas into the theory of core and optional sleep. Core sleep consists of stages 3 and 4 SWS and REM, and is essential for restoring the brain to an optimum level of function. According to Horne, Stages 1 and 2 of slow wave sleep (SWS) are not essential and are referred to as optional sleep. Bodily restoration occurs during optional sleep and during periods of relaxed wakefulness.

Evaluation of restoration theories

The restoration theories are highly testable, so there is a lot of evidence to back the assumptions put forward by such people as Oswald and Horne:

➤ In animal studies Everson et al (1989) found that rats that were sleep deprived had an increased metabolic rate and a dramatic loss in weight, and died within 19 days. If the rats were allowed to sleep a little, death was prevented. This suggests that sleep is vital and restorative, as the rat's symptoms were relieved by sleep. However, it is not possible to tell what caused the symptoms: the sleep deprivation or the stress of being constantly stimulated to stay awake.

➤ Stern & Morgane (1974) found that when people were deprived of REM sleep, they would go straight into a deep sleep and gain the REM sleep they lost previously (REM rebound). Their bodies and minds sought restoration. In contrast, people who were on anti-depressant medication, which may cause insomnia, did not have this REM rebound when they came off medication. Stern & Morgane suggested; it was possibly due to the drugs causing an increase of neurotransmitters, such as serotonin, so rebound was unnecessary. This would imply that the neurotransmitters are linked to the reason why we sleep.

Arguments against restoration theories include the following:

➤ If Oswald's idea that SWS restores body tissue is correct, then a person who has run a marathon, for instance, should sleep for longer in order to restore their body, but this is not the case. The person may fall asleep faster, but they will not sleep proportionately to the amount they have exerted their body.

➤ Horne (1988) analysed 50 studies on sleep deprivation and found very few had their physical performance affected or showed signs of stress from the sleep deprivation, contradicting Oswald's idea that SWS was necessary for body restoration.

➤ Horne also suggested that the idea of growth in SWS stage 4 was questionable, as the protein synthesis needed for this to happen would be minimal. This is because amino acids (needed for the protein synthesis) are only available for up to 5 hours after eating and most people do not eat for a while before going to bed.

Brain plasticity theory

More recently, the theory of brain plasticity has gained in popularity, leading to an increase in research in the area, e.g. Myamoto & Hensch (2003) and Ribeiro (2012). Brain plasticity suggests the brain is plastic (malleable) and modifies to consolidate and assimilate new information during sleep.

The theory suggests that neurons (nerves cells) in the brain are constantly rearranging themselves in order to fit in new neurons or to change the connections of existing neurons (Benington & Frank 2003). This reconfiguring happens during sleep, with some connections increasing in strength and others disappearing altogether if no longer useful. This process helps memory consolidation in long-term memory (LTM) and learning. It is thought the process needs to take place during sleep when there are no external stimuli that need attending to and no need to control behaviour.

Cohen (1979) suggested that two predictions could be made using brain plasticity as a function of sleep.

1. That LTM should improve after sleep

2. If there is sleep deprivation, then LTM should be impaired.

Research supporting the brain plasticity theory
Marquet et al. (2000) found that when humans learned a new thing, it triggered a specific part of brain activation. They later observed the same area of brain activation takes place during REM sleep. This demonstrated there was practice taking place during REM sleep, suggesting that there is an amalgamation of LTM traces in REM sleep.

Research contradicting the brain plasticity theory
Dement (1974) and Meddis (1977) reported cases of people who only habitually slept 3–4 hours and 1 hour in a 24-hour time period, yet both still functioned perfectly well and lived into old age.

Case study: fatal familial insomnia

There are some families who have a genetic mutation that causes them to develop a condition called fatal familial insomnia. People with this condition sleep normally until the onset of middle age, but then develop chronic insomnia (cannot sleep) and generally die within two years of the start of their insomnia. Post-mortem (after-death) examinations show a cause as the degeneration of the thalamus. This supports the restoration theory of sleep, but as the occurrence of this condition is rare and the numbers of people examined so small, results cannot be generalised.

References

EVERSON, C. A. et al (1989) Sleep Deprivation in the Rat: III. Total Sleep Deprivation. *Sleep*. 12. pp.13–21.

MARQUET, P. et al (2000) Experience-Dependent Changes in Cerebral Activation during Human REM Sleep. *Nature Neuroscience*. 3. pp.831–6.

MIYAMOTO, H. & HENSCH, T. K. (2003) 'Reciprocal interaction of sleep and synaptic plasticity', www.ncbi.nlm.nih.gov/pubmed/14993461 [retrieved August 2012]

RIBEIRO, S. J. (2012) Sleep and plasticity. *Pflugers Arch*. January; 463 (1). pp.111–20.

STERN, W. C. & MORGANE, P. J. (1974) Theoretical View of REM Sleep: Maintenance of Catecholamine Systems in the Central Nervous System. *Behavioral Biology*. 11. pp.1–32.

Social learning theory

Social learning theory (SLT) was introduced by Bandura and Walters (1959) and is often classed as a neo-behaviourist model, as it puts forward the idea that memory is involved in learning. The basic idea is a person, such as a child will look to others they respect or want to be like (model), then store and later imitate their actions. They are more likely to follow the model's behaviour if it has been rewarded, or at least nothing adverse has resulted from it.

Bandura's ideas on aggression

Bandura and others believed that children are not born with an aggressive nature, but rather become aggressive because of their environment. Through observation, the child will look up to models, such as parents, peers and sports stars. They will see how the models act and what the consequences of their actions are.

Bandura defined the difference between *learning* behaviour from a model and *performing* the behaviour that was learnt. Whether or not a child goes on to imitate the behaviour depends on the possible outcomes:

➤ If the consequences are good for the model, the child gains vicarious reinforcement – a type of indirect reinforcement that makes it more likely that the child will imitate the behaviour to get a similar reward.

➤ If the model is punished for their behaviour, then it is not likely to be imitated, but the behaviour will still have been learnt.

See also:
Approaches:
behavioural.

Research: Bandura's Bobo doll studies

Bandura et al. (1961) carried out a study using 72 children (36 boys and 36 girls) with a mean average age of just over 4 years. The children were put into one of three conditions (12 male and 12 female in each group). They were also all matched for pre-existing levels of aggression,

as that was the behaviour being tested. There were two experimental groups:

➤ Aggressive model – where the children witnessed an adult being physically and verbally abusive towards a Bobo doll (a large inflatable doll).

➤ Non-aggressive model – where the children witnessed an adult acting neutrally toward the Bobo doll.

The third group was a control group, where there was no model shown. All children spent some time in a room where they were not allowed to play with attractive toys, and then were then put into a room with the Bobo doll.

Findings
The children who had witnessed the aggressive role model, displayed significantly more aggression when left in the room with the Bobo doll than the other two groups. The researchers concluded that children do seem to learn aggressive behaviour from their role models. Boys were more likely to imitate male role models in physical and verbal aggression and gun play. Girls were more likely to imitate female role models in verbal aggression, though this was not a significant result.

Research: vicarious reinforcement (Bandura 1965)

In 1965, Bandura designed another study to test the effect of vicarious reinforcement – that is, whether the child's imitation of a model's behaviour was dependent on what happened to the model. The children were put into three groups and all three saw the model being aggressive. One group saw the model rewarded for the aggression. One group saw the model punished and the third group saw the model experience no particular consequences for their behaviour.

Results showed that the group who had seen the model rewarded were more likely to imitate the model's behaviour than the other two groups. However, if the children in all groups were offered a reward for imitating the behaviour, there was a high level of imitation. This shows the children who had seen the model punished had chosen not to imitate due to the negative outcome, this is where the model has a cognitive element.

Case study: gender role models

A brother and sister grow up in a family where the father frequently verbally and physically abuses their mother. He is never punished for his behaviour, and their mother has a quieter life if she acts subordinately. The boy grows up to abuse his own wife, while the daughter becomes an abused wife. SLT explains this in terms of the children being more likely to imitate same gender behaviour:

As the father has not been punished, the son is more likely to see this as the way to behave to his wife.

Seeing her mother being subordinate and rewarded for that by not being abused, the daughter is likely to imitate her behaviour.

Reciprocal determinism

This is where learning from others determines behaviour and therefore a past experience which has been stored will affect present behaviour. The reciprocal aspect comes in with the idea that as an individual acts, this in turn causes a change in the environment, which will in turn affect subsequent behaviour e.g. if you watch someone carrying out a task, such as taking notes in class and then you imitate them, this will cause modification in that person's behaviour, which will in turn affect your behaviour too. People are also quite able to make their own choice whether to imitate or not.

Self-efficacy

This is where a person can affect their own outcome of behaviour, which will be a sense of one's own effectiveness e.g. if you believe you can pass an exam, you will approach the task differently than if you felt you would not be able to, which will bring about the desired outcome of passing the exam. Self-efficacy can result from both direct and indirect experience. Direct experience is where that person's own successes or failures will influence future expectations of success and indirect is where the experiences of others around you will have an impact on whether you think you can succeed or fail.

Social Cognitive Theory (SCT)

Bandura's later studies saw SLT evolve into Social Cognitive Theory (SCT), a more cognitive-based theory. The cognitive aspect focuses on whether the person *chooses* to imitate behaviour by assessing whether it is a good idea to carry it out. This decision will be based on that person's experience and reasoning, along with the reactions of others to the behaviour.

Evaluation

SLT goes beyond the simplicity of conditioning principles and offers a more complex and robust explanation of human behaviour, allowing for both nature (cognitive function) and nurture (experiences).

Memory (storing of experiences of others and ways in which to deal with a given situation), observation, imitation and modelling, all require cognitive capacity, as they are processes of the mind. SLT also accounts for cultural and individual differences, as the individual creates a unique mental store of behaviour from their experiences.

A problem with SLT is when it comes to make assumptions, that if a person experiences a given behaviour or situation, they will in turn imitate that behaviour if vicariously reinforced, but not all do choose to imitate that behaviour. Bandura's incorporation of reciprocal determinism and self-efficacy though does seem to answer the previous point, in that a person can choose what they imitate.

References

BANDURA, A. (1965) Influence of Models' Reinforcement Contingencies on the Acquisition of Imitative Responses. *Journal of Personality and Social Psychology.* 1 (6). pp.589–95.

BANDURA, A., ROSS, D. & ROSS, S. A. (1961) Transmission of Aggression Through Imitation of Aggressive Models. *Journal of Abnormal and Social Psychology.* 63. pp.575–82.

BANDURA, A. & WALTERS, R. H. (1959) *Adolescent Aggression.* New York: Ronald.

Stress: bodily responses

The bodily response to stress involves the endocrine system (a network of glands that release hormones and neurotransmitters, such as adrenaline and nor-adrenaline) and the autonomic nervous system (ANS). The ANS consists of two branches: the sympathetic and parasympathetic branch. The endocrine system and ANS work in synchronization to prepare the body for whatever challenge is presented.

Two response pathways

Selye (1936) suggested there are two bodily response pathways to stress. These are:

➤ the sympathomedullary (or acute) pathway, which gives the person extra resources to fight the stress as it happens, or to flee from it.

➤ the pituitary-adrenal pathway, which supplies the energy needed to continue coping with the stressor for a longer period.

These response pathways are summarised in the diagram. When the brain detects a stressor, it will trigger the hypothalamus, which activates both pathways at the same time. The hypothalamus acts as a kind of control centre and plays a vital role in controlling many bodily functions.

Bodily response to stress

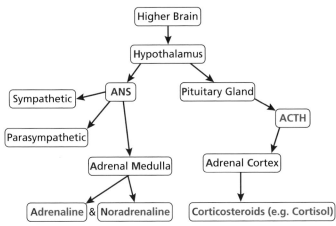

Sympathomedullary pathway

Triggering of the sympathomedullary results in the sympathetic branch of the ANS being activated, causing excitation; heart rate and sweating increase rapidly, for example. The ANS also causes the adrenal medulla (part of the adrenal gland, near the kidneys) to release adrenaline (an arousal hormone) and noradrenaline. The combination of excitation of the sympathetic branch and the energy surge of adrenaline gives the person increased strength, enabling them either to run away (flight) or stay and deal with the situation (fight).

After a while, the parasympathetic branch of the ANS calms down the excitation in the sympathetic branch. (As an analogy, sympathetic branch can be thought of as the accelerator and the parasympathetic branch as the brake.) Noradrenaline calms the adrenaline's effects, so the fight or flight response is no longer available.

This response can be remembered by the acronym HANSAMAN – see the letters coloured red in the diagram.

Pituitary–adrenal pathway

The pituitary gland is a small gland in the brain, the size of a pea, that plays an important role in regulating vital body functions. As the pituitary–adrenal pathway is triggered, the hypothalamus indirectly causes the pituitary gland to release adrenocortioctrophic hormone (ACTH). This in turn triggers the adrenal cortex to release corticosteroids (stress hormones), including cortisol. When the corticosteroids are in the blood stream, they cause the liver to release fatty acids, providing the energy to continue dealing with the stressor. This is the pathway that is most associated with chronic stress and illness (see 'Exhaustion' below).

This response can be remembered by the acronym HPACC –refer to the letters coloured red in the diagram.

Case study: reacting to a stressful situation

Dan is in a car crash, where another person is trapped under his car. Dan is able to pull himself out of his own car and lift the other person's car far enough for him to get out. When the emergency services arrive, they find Dan has managed to do this with a broken leg.

Dan's actions can be explained by referring to the pathways. In the first few minutes of the accident happening, Dan's sympatho-medullary pathway was activated, releasing adrenaline and so giving him the increased strength to help the other driver. Later, after the parasympathetic branch of the ANS was activated and noradrenaline calmed down the effects of the adrenaline, Dan felt the effects of his injuries. He now has corticosteroids in his body (released by the pituitary–adrenal system), helping him deal with the effects of his injuries.

Selye's General Adaptation Syndrome (GAS)

Hans Selye (1936, 1950) put together a framework of the bodily responses to a stressor, using the bodily response pathways. He called this the General Adaptation Syndrome (GAS). This model was suggested after his studies on rats and animals. He found, no matter what the stressor was, from exposure to noxious gas to cutting off a limb, it always resulted in the same response. The GAS model has three stages:

Alarm
A stressor is detected and the body goes into the sympathomedullary response, where fight or flight is possible. There is also the start of the pituitary–adrenal pathway response, releasing cortisol.

Resistance
As the body has to provide a way with coping effectively with an ongoing stressor, the pituitary–adrenal pathway

continues to produce corticosteroids, allowing the release of fatty acids from the liver into the bloodstream. These supply the energy needed to resist the stressor. The sympathomedullary pathway will have stopped its response.

Exhaustion

This occurs as hormone reserves are reduced and the body can no longer keep up with normal functioning. The sympathetic branch of the ANS will possibly give out symptoms, such as sweating and raised heart rate. If the stressor is long-lasting or chronic, the body may show symptoms of stress-related illness, e.g. ulcers, depression and heart problems, as the bodily responses can induce both physical and psychological responses.

References

SELYE, H. (1936) A Syndrome Produced by Diverse Nocuous Agents. *Nature*. 138. pp.32.

SELYE, H. (1950) Stress. *Acta*, Montreal.

Stress: individual differences

There are variations in how people perceive and cope with stress, which will in turn influence the effects of stress on them. Some people feel and suffer stress much more acutely than others. The reasons for these individual differences include personality type, the hardiness of a person, their locus of control and their manner of coping (emotion or problem-focused).

The individual differences referred to here can be applied to all areas of research in psychology.

Transactional model of stress

The model shows that stress occurs when there is a mismatch between perceived demands and perceived ability to cope (Lazarus & Folkman, 1974). The ability to cope depends on past experience and type of personality.

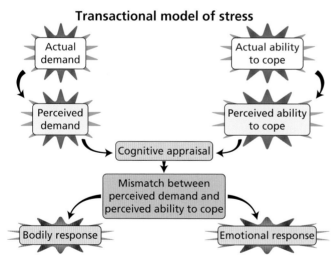

Transactional model of stress

Type of personality

Friedman and Rosenham (1959) found that Type A people were twice as likely to suffer coronary heart disease (CHD) than Type B, suggesting much higher stress levels. Type A people are motivated, competitive and often aggressive, with low levels of patience and tolerance. Type B people are the opposite and seem to feel stress a lot less acutely. (In reality, most people are a mixture of the two types, and are known as Type X.)

Hardy personality

A person with a hardy personality tends to cope with stress well. In Kobasa's study (1979) of executives undergoing stress at work, she found people with hardy personalities were 50% less likely to suffer illness from stress. The hardy personality she suggested consists of the 3 Cs: challenge, control and commitment. Features are:

➤ Seeing a problem as a challenge rather than a threat.

➤ Taking control of the situation by employing strategies to deal with the challenge and then will

➤ Stay committed to dealing with the situation by employing various methods of coping, because they have a meaning and purpose in life. This commitment means they keep on striving.

Hardy people generally have a range of coping strategies. One of the psychological therapies to treat stress is hardiness training, a form of cognitive behavioural therapy (CBT) that helps the person to see situations differently.

Locus of control

This concerns where the centre of control lies in a person's life, being either internal or external (Rotter, 1954).

A person with a high internal locus of control will take complete responsibility for their own thoughts, feelings and behaviour. They will suffer or enjoy the consequences of their behaviour and will be self-reliant, putting no blame on others either real or imagined. They are less likely to suffer the consequences of stress as much as someone who has an external locus of control – though someone at the extreme end of the spectrum may have a tendency to be a control freak, which can cause stress.

A person with a high external locus of control feels they have no control over their own lives and is likely to blame everyone except themselves for their failures and luck for their successes. They are unlikely to accept any responsibility for their actions and will blame someone or something else if possible. At the extreme, they will spend their lives being a victim of circumstance. They may develop feelings of hopelessness and helplessness, making them more susceptible to depression and to suffer the effects of stress in a more intense and chronic way emotionally.

Types of coping

Folkman & Lazarus (1990) suggested two ways in which people deal with stressful situations: emotion focused coping (EFC) and problem focused coping (PFC).

An EFC person will focus on the emotions surrounding a stressful event or situation, they will not deal with the problem at hand. A person using EPC will often use a variety of defence mechanisms to divert from the problem, including denial. For example, a person experiencing financial difficulties may put letters from the bank in a drawer unopened.

A PFC person will evolve a strategy to deal with the stressor. For example, if told they have a serious illness, someone using PFC will research everything they can about the illness, then put strategies in place to cope with it.

Most people use a combination of both types of coping.

Research: Western Collaborate study (1959)

In this study Friedman & Rosenham set out to support their idea that Type A people had a higher risk of developing heart disease. The study looked at around 3000 healthy American men, aged between 39 and 59, and found after eight years, the men classed as Type A were twice as likely to have died of a heart attack or to have a higher rate of heart disease than Type B. They were also more likely to engage in bad lifestyle choices, such as smoking, and had significantly higher blood pressure and cholesterol levels. These findings therefore supported the research idea.

However, other researchers carried out follow-up studies. Ragland & Brand (1988) found that, in total, 214 men from the 3000 originally studied had died of heart disease. They concluded that this only supported the idea that age, lifestyle habits and high blood pressure were contributory to heart disease, but that no direct evidence linked Type A personality and heart disease risk. Myrtek (2001) carried out a meta-analysis, which found a link with the hostility characteristic of Type A and heart disease, but no other evidence to link Type A personality and heart disease.

Case study: stress at college

Close to her exams, Anna, a college student, became erratic, losing weight and having endless headaches, due to a mismatch between the perceived demand and her perceived ability to cope. Another student, Bella, viewed the exams with a degree of positive expectation, seeing them as a finale to her consistent work (cognitive appraisal). She was aware that her exam success would correlate directly with her effort, and saw exams as a surmountable challenge. So there was a degree of stress (good stress). Hans Selye (1954) termed this 'eustress'; later developed by Lazarus, (1996).

It is clear that a particular demand can cause different degrees of stress, depending on the individual's perception. It was useful for Bella to have some stress, because it helped her to achieve her goals.

It is evident from the above that there are not only physiological responses from the endocrine and autonomic nervous systems, but that emotions and behaviours are also involved. For Anna there was anxiety and erratic behaviour, eating disruption and illness. For Bella, there was mild good stress, which motivated her to work consistently and diligently. Bella can be classed as using problem-focused coping and having a high internal locus of control.

References

FOLKMAN, S. & LAZARUS, R. S. (1990) Coping and Emotion. In STEIN, N. et al (eds.) *Psychological and Biological Approaches to Emotion.* London: Psychology Press.

FRIEDMAN, M. & ROSENMAN, R. (1959) Association of Specific Overt Behaviour Pattern with Blood and Cardiovascular Findings. *Journal of the American Medical Association.* 169. pp.1286–96.

KOBASA, S. C. (1979). Stressful Life Events, Personality, and Health – Inquiry into Hardiness. *Journal of Personality and Social Psychology.* 37 (1). pp.1–11.

LAZARUS, R. S. (1966) *Psychological Stress and the Coping Process.* New York, Toronto, London: McGraw-Hill Book Co.

LAZARUS, R. S. & Folkman, S. (1974). *Stress, Appraisal and Coping.* New York: Springer.

MYRTEK, M. (2001) Meta-analysis of Prospective Studies on Coronary Heart Disease, Type A Personality and Hostility. *International Journal of Cardiology.* 79. pp.245–51.

RAGLAND, D. R. & BRAND, R. J. (1988), Type A behaviour and Mortality from Coronary Heart Disease. *New England Journal of Medicine.* 318 (2). pp.65–9.

ROTTER, J. B. (1954). *Social Learning and Clinical Psychology.* NY: Prentice-Hall.

SELYE, H. (1974). *Stress Without Distress.* 171. Philadelphia: J.B. Lippincott Company.

Stress: workplace

Workplace stress is simply stress that is caused by your job, wherever that takes place. Four main sources of stress have been identified with regard to the workplace: physical environment, work overload, lack of control, and role conflict.

Sources of stress

The following table summarises some of the sources of stress in the workplace and the research that has been conducted into these reasons for stress.

Source of stress	Research
Physical environment Includes factors such as physical work environment i.e. temperature, noise and work space. Environmental factors are known to relate to an increase in aggression.	In support of this, Glass et al (1969) tested the effect of noise on student performance of a cognitive task, using physiological measurements such as GSR (galvanic skin response – sweat) in either noise or no noise environment. They found as noise increased, so did irritation, concluding that noise has a negative effect on stress levels.
Work overload This is when a person has too many demands in a limited space of time, leading to a feeling of relentless demand and inability to ever get finished. This intrudes on areas of life, other than work, causing symptoms such as disturbed sleep.	Dewe (1992) defined the term home-work interface to describe the negative effect on home life, when a person suffers work overload, after finding families spent far too much time apart due to the pressure of work tasks. More recently, Pearson (2008) found work overload to be the most important factor when looking at the psychological health of 155 working women. Work overload was found to be negatively correlated to psychological health and job satisfaction.

Lack of control	Marmot et at (1997) investigated the demands of work and the effects of low control on 7372 civil servants. The workers answered a questionnaire and were tested for heart disease. The researchers found a lack of control had a more significant effect on people's health than high job demand did.
This is about how much control a person has over their working life, or indeed any aspect of life. Most people's working hours are determined by their employers, resulting in a loss of control and feelings of powerlessness. However, not all people react negatively to a lack of control.	
	Schaubroeck et al (2001) did find that some less-stressed people have a better immune response when in situations of low control.
Role conflict and ambiguity	A study by Quah et al (1994) had 144 respondents, who had an average of three years' management experience, mostly of Chinese ethnicity (94%) with 72% male and 28% female population. The method consisted of; Rizzo et al (1970) 14 item scale on role conflict and ambiguity, along with questionnaires. The findings showed there was a significant and positive link demonstrated by Singaporean managers from role conflict and ambiguity in the workplace. They also found work stress had a significant negative effect on job satisfaction levels.
Role conflict arises when a person has the responsibilities of more than one role and those responsibilities do not blend well, for example needing to stay late at work and family responsibilities.	
Ambiguity arises when a lack of clear direction leads to a person being unsure of what they should be doing. It may lead to conflict with other workers and bosses. The person may over-compensate and try to do everything, leading to work overload and lack of control.	

References

DEWE, P. J. (1992) Applying the Concept of Appraisal to Work Stressors: Some Exploratory Analysis. *Human Relations*. 45. pp.143–64.

GLASS, D. C. et al (1969) Psychic Cost of Adaptation to an Environmental Stressor. *Journal of Personality and Social Psychology*. 12. pp.200–10.

MARMOT, M. et al (1997) Contribution of Job Control and Other Risk Factors to Social Variation in Health Disease Incidence. *The Lancet*. 350. pp.235–9.

PEARSON, Q. M. (2008) Role Overload, Job Satisfaction, Leisure Satisfaction, and Psychological Health among Employed Women. *Journal of Counseling and Development*. January 1, 2008.

QUAH, J. & CAMPBELL, K. M. (1994). Role Conflict and Role Ambiguity as Factors in Work Stress among Managers in Singapore: Some Moderator Variables, *Research and Practice in Human Resource Management*. 2(1). pp.21–33.

SCHAUBROECK, J. et al (2001) Individual Difference in Utilizing Control to Cope with Job Demands: Effects on Susceptibility to Infectious Disease. *Journal of Applied Psychology*. 86(2). pp.265–78.

SHIROM, A. (1989) Burnout in Work Organisations. In COOPER, C. L. & ROBERTSON, I. (eds.) *International Review of Industrial and Organisational Psychology*. Chichester, UK: Wiley.

Therapies: behavioural

Behavioural therapies used to treat psychopathology (psychological disorders) reflect the ideas behind this approach. Several of them are based on classical and operant conditioning. They include aversion therapy, systematic desensitisation, flooding and token economy.

Therapies based on classical conditioning

Aversion therapy

This is used mainly to treat addiction to alcohol, other drugs or any unwanted forms of behaviour. The aim is to remove undesirable behaviour by associating it with a negative stimulus. For example, an emetic (drug that causes vomiting) could be given to an alcoholic every time they have an alcoholic drink. The emetic is the aversion stimulus; the vomiting will be associated with drinking alcohol and will hopefully in due course lead to the person ceasing to drink alcohol. The therapy can be presented as follows:

See also:
Conditioning:
classical.

Aversion therapy has met with some success but there are ethical issues linked to using emetics. The emetic has also sometimes been paired with an electric shock, to intensify the negative association with the undesirable behaviour. Such stimuli may cause pain and suffering (Howard, 2001). As a result, there is a high drop-out rate. An extreme dramatisation of aversion therapy can be seen in Stanley Kubrick's film *Clockwork Orange* (Certificate 18: contains some harrowing adult content).

Psychology

Systematic desensitisation (Wolpe, 1969)

This therapy was originally developed for people suffering from post-traumatic stress sisorder (PTSD), but has proved to be very successful in the treatment of phobias. The aim is to change the undesirable behaviour by substituting a different response (relaxation) to the stimulus. This is achieved via a series of systematic steps, each of which exposes the client to a low level of their fear stimulus until they are just out of their comfort zone. They are then helped to relax again. The stimulus then moves to the next level of fear. The process continues until the client has reached the top of their agreed **hierarchy of fear.**

The therapy has generally proved successful, especially as the client has a high level of control over the desensitisation process. Problems include:

➤ the client not being honest about the level of fear, so the hierarchy is not appropriate

➤ the client finding it difficult to relax on demand, as relaxation is a contradiction to the stress response.

Implosion/flooding

These similar therapies are both methods of **forced reality**, where the client is submerged completely in their fear. The aim is to eradicate the fear by a prolonged and continuous presentation of the feared object (such as spiders for arachnophobia) or situation (such as open spaces for agoraphobia). The fear is thought to be eradicated by an eventual acclimatisation, so that the fear responses reach a stable point, then disappear. This will **lead to a reduction in anxiety** and other emotions connected with the phobic response.

With implosion, the phobic is asked to imagine and live through their worst fear – a mental ordeal. In flooding, the feared object or situation is actually present – a physical ordeal.

194

Both methods are known to be effective, but flooding more so than implosion (Wolpe, 1958 and Boulougouris & Marks, 1969). They are also long-lasting, time-efficient and cheap. Problems include:

➤ the possibility of a vulnerable person having a heart attack

➤ the opposite desired effect being achieved, as the person pulls out of therapy and the phobia intensifies.

Therapies based on operant conditioning

Behaviour shaping (Skinner, 1953)

This uses successive reinforcements leading to the ultimate desired behaviour. It was first carried out in the laboratory, using pigeons. A series of rewards is given, so that a particular desired behaviour is rewarded but then the next stage in the series of desired behaviours must be achieved in order for the next reward to be earned. Skinner trained pigeons to play ping pong with their beaks by firstly rewarding them with food when they pecked at the ball. In order to get the reward again, the birds had to tap the ball across to the other pigeon, with the ultimate desired behaviour being for them to be playing in real time.

This type of therapy can be used to mould young children's behaviour and is very popular for training animals, such as dogs. However, it is limited in its use with humans and is ineffective for serious psychotic illness, such as schizophrenia.

Selective positive reinforcement

This rewards only the desired behaviour and actually denies rewards if the behaviour is not shown. Stunkard (1972) use this method with anorexic and obese patients, where treats like watching TV and personal time would be withheld until the desired behaviour (eating normally) took place.

Token economy

This method of behaviour modification works by rewarding the desired behaviour with a token. The token is a secondary reinforcer, which can be exchanged for a primary reinforcer later, such as a treat. The method works well in a particular environment, such as a prison or school. Any paid employment represents a sort of token economy, with the desired behaviour (work) being rewarded with money, but the best example is performance-related pay.

The therapy has wide-ranging uses from treating people with substance abuse (Lewis, 2008) to an effective, evidence based, psychological treatment for the secondary effects of institutionalisation in schizophrenia (Shean, 2008)

A weakness is that the learnt behaviour may not endure when the person leaves the particular environment.

Case study: systematic desensitisation

A person with a phobia, such as arachnophobia (fear of spiders) meets with the therapist, who gains information about the patient's level of fear, including its severity and intensity. With the patient's agreement, the therapist creates a hierarchy of fear situations. Before the desensitisation treatment begins, the therapist will teach the phobic relaxation techniques and give them time to practise them with scenarios.

The desensitisation process takes the phobic from their lowest level of fear, which might be to be to hear the word spider, to their highest level of fear, in progressive steps. At each step, the therapist takes the arachnophobic to a place of discomfort, then encourages them to use relaxation techniques so as to get back to a feeling of relative comfort.

This process goes on until the person can face the phobia at very close proximity, such as having the spider crawl on their hand (top level of the hierarchy), without feeling the irrational fear. This enables them to stop being phobic to the point that disrupts their everyday life and their fear may just become a dislike.

References

BOULOUGOURIS, J. C. & MARKS, I. M. (1969) Implosion (Flooding)—A New Treatment for Phobias. *British Medical Journal*. June 21; 2 (5659). pp.721–3.

HOWARD, M. (2001) Pharmacological Aversion Treatment of Alcohol Abuse. *American Journal of Drug and Alcohol Abuse*. 27 (3). pp.561–85.

LEWIS, M. L. (2008) Application of Contingency Management-Prize Reinforcement to Community Practice with Alcohol and Drug Problems: A critical Examination. *Behaviour and Social Issues.*, 17. pp.119–38.

SHEAN, G. D. (2009) Evidence-based Psychosocial Practices and Recovery from Schizophrenia. *Psychiatry*. 72. pp.307–20.

STUNKARD, A. (1972) New Therapies for the Eating Disorders. Behavior Modification of Obesity and Anorexia Nervosa. *Archives of General Psychiatry*. 26 (5). pp.391–8.

WOLPE, J. (1969) *The Practice of Behavior Therapy*. London: Pergamon Press.

Therapies: biological

Biological therapies treat disorders according to the medical model. The client is assessed for symptoms, diagnosed and then treated appropriately. The therapies derive from the various causes of disorder in the biological approach, which include biochemical, brain structure and micro-organism. They include drugs and electro-convulsive therapy (ECT).

Drug therapy (chemotherapy)

Drugs are now the most common form of biological therapy. They work on the nervous system by balancing neurotransmitters and hormones. There are three main categories:

➤ Anxiolytics, more commonly known as anti-anxiety drugs. These are minor tranquillisers used to treat people with disorders such as phobias, panic attacks and OCD.

➤ Anti-depressants, with the sub-categories of MAOIs, SSRIs, SSNIs and tricyclics, used to treat people with uni-polar depression.

➤ Anti-psychotics, major tranquilisers used to treat people with psychotic symptoms, most commonly with schizophrenic patients. There are two types: typical, which only treat positive symptoms (delusions and hallucinations) and atypical, which treat positive and negative symptoms, such as poverty of speech.

Strengths

➤ They are easy to use and efficient at alleviating symptoms.

➤ They are more cost- and time-efficient than psychotherapy.

Weaknesses

➤ There are side effects, ranging from minor effects, such as insomnia with drugs that reduce the availability of serotonin (anti-anxiety), to major effects, such as symptoms resembling schizophrenia with typical anti-psychotic drugs.

➤ There are some problems with effectiveness, due to patients either not wanting to take a drug because of side effects or being unreliable in taking the drugs.

➤ Patients may become tolerant of the drug, needing a higher dose to achieve the same result.

➤ Patient may become dependent on the drug as a security blanket.

➤ Drugs only relieve symptoms, so the problem remains unless other treatments, such as psychotherapy, are used in combination.

Electro-convulsive therapy (ECT)

This highly controversial treatment is thought to reconfigure the biochemical balance of the brain. It is most commonly used for extreme cases of depression.

It started as an experimental treatment for patients with schizophrenia and had little success, but therapists did notice its effectiveness with depressed patients and it is now recommended for use in a limited way for clinical depression and for schizophrenia in USA and UK. The procedure involves passing an electrical current through one or both of the temples of the brain. There are fewer side effects when only the non-dominant side of the brain (one temple) has the current. Prior to the electrical charge, the patient is given a combination of drugs that alleviate body convulsion and relax the muscles.

The charge causes a seizure, which is thought to reconfigure the chemicals and neurons in the brain, though there is still debate over how it actually works. Treatments vary from USA to UK, but generally take place over a 2–6 week period, though maintenance shocks are also given in some cases. The USA tend to give shocks more often but for a shorter time.

Strengths

➤ It has worked for around 60% of depressed patients who have responded to no other treatment, enabling them to have a better quality of life.

➤ When it works, it is fast and efficient at relieving severe symptoms.

Weaknesses

➤ Side effects, such as, memory loss and confusion. The confusion will subside, but the memory loss is permanent (Lisenby et al, 2000).

➤ It may cause cognitive dysfunction, which supports the idea that the treatment results in brain damage (Sackheim et al, 2007), although those who believe in ECT dispute this vehemently.

➤ Standard risks associated with the use of anaesthetic.

➤ The relapse rate is very high, usually within six months of the treatment.

➤ There are ethical issues, as it is sometimes done without the patient's consent (Rose et al, 2007), although the World Health Organisation states there should always be consent given (WHO, 2005).

Psychosurgery

Psychosurgery is used very infrequently and in some countries is banned altogether, as it is highly controversial. The US and UK do use it occasionally for disorders such as OCD and severe depression (Neurosurgery working group, 2000). It involves destroying a small amount of connective tissue in the frontal lobes of the brain. Brain scans and precision tools, such as electrical current or radioactive pellets, make the procedure more precise and focused than it used to be.

If the surgery works, it is a fast and effective treatment, but the risks of brain damage are very high.

Research

Placebos are often used when testing the efficacy of a drug, as they mimic a real treatment but have no treatment value. Kirsch & Saperstein (2008) did a meta-analysis on clinical trials of an anti-depressant drug and found that, while the placebo effect was high, the drug effect was modest. As a result, Kirsch then carried out a meta-analysis of both published and unpublished trials into anti-depressants from the US Food and Drug Administration and found the difference between the placebo and the anti-depressant drugs was not clinically significant. This was according to the standard the NHS uses, published by NICE (*National Institute for Health and Clinical Excellence*) (Kirsch et al, 2010). These findings have caused a great deal of controversy, as they cast doubt on the whole theory that depression is caused by a chemical imbalance.

Case study: psychosurgery

In 1998, Mary Lou Zimmerman underwent brain surgery at the Cleveland Clinic, to relieve the symptoms of severe OCD. Four lesions were created in her brain by heated electrodes. Irreversible damage was caused to the brain tissue. Mary's symptoms included being unable to talk and emotional disability, including dementia. In 2002, she was awarded damages of $7.5 million, as the court found the Clinic guilty of gross negligence. They were also found guilty of not informing the family of the potential dangers involved in this highly risky and experimental procedure.

Due to this case, many projects involving psychosurgery have been axed, leading to a decline in psychosurgery.

References

KIRSCH, I. (2010). *The Emperor's New Drugs: Exploding the Antidepressant Myth*. New York: Basic Books.

LISANBY, S. H., MADDOX, J. H., PRUDIC, J., DEVANAND, D. P., SACKEIM, H. A. (June 2000). The Effects of Electroconvulsive Therapy on Memory of Autobiographical and Public Events. *Arch. General. Psychiatry,* 57 (6). pp.581–90.

NEUROSURGERY WORKING GROUP (2000) *Neurosurgery for Mental Disorder*. London: Royal College of Psychiatrists.

SACKEIM, H. A., PRUDIC, J., FULLER, R., KEILP, J., LAVORI, P. W., OLFSON, M. (January 2007). The Cognitive Effects of Electroconvulsive Therapy in Community Settings. *Neuropsychopharmacology.* 32 (1). pp.244–54.

TEW, Jr., J. D., MULSANT, B. H., HASKETT, R. F., JOAN, P., BEGLEY., A. E., SACKEIM, H. A. (2007). Relapse during Continuation Pharmacotherapy after Acute Response to ECT: A Comparison of Usual Care versus Protocolized Treatment. *Annals of Clinical Psychiatry.* 19 (1). pp.1–4.

Therapies: CBT

Cognitive-behavioural therapy (CBT) originates from the cognitive approach. It was created by a cognitive psychotherapist, Aaron Beck (1967). It links to the behavioural approach in that it is based on the idea that behaviour can be changed. A precursor to CBT was Ellis's rational-emotive behaviour therapy (REBT 1962). The two therapies are similar but focus on slightly different aspects of cognitive thinking.

The theory behind the therapies

It is thought people process information in a maladaptive way, which distorts their view of people and situations. This results in an irrational and negative view, which then translates into maladaptive behaviour.

Therapy from this approach seeks to correct the client's perception into positive and rational views. Ellis suggested that irrational thinking was natural, but also believed people had the power to radically alter their perceptions of the world for the better, which would lead to Improved mental health and behaviour.

Both therapies come from the idea that whenever there is an event, the mind will process this and it will affect how the person deals with it. Ellis's ABC model is such a process: There is an activating event such as an exam, which triggers a belief of some sort. The way the person perceives and evaluates the event then has a direct effect on the consequences of the event – their actions.

Beck's contribution to CBT was to pioneer the use of this new interactive therapy and develop scientific tests to see if the treatment worked, such as the depression inventory and the Beck's anxiety inventory, these were standardised tests that measured subjective feelings of depression (also see Beck's Cognitive triad in the Cognitive approach).

In CBT, the therapist is helping the client change their inference of a situation. In REBT, the therapist is helping the client to change their core belief. Both are forms of psychotherapy, working to change negative and irrational thinking into positive and rational thinking, and so a positive change in behaviour. Other therapies that can be termed cognitive-behavioural include Stress Inoculation Therapy (SIT) introduced by Meichenbaum and Hardiness training developed by Kobasa, both used to treat stress.

Difference between REBT and CBT

Each of these therapies is slightly different. For example, the table below shows the thought process each therapy deals with, when helping a student receiving disappointing exam results.

CBT: Inference	REBT: Core belief	Evaluation
I will never amount to anything.'	'I have to be successful.'	'I am worthless' – which will lead to a lack of effort and feelings of inadequacy
With CBT, the inference will be disputed, with the rational argument: 'This is just one exam and it is still possible to be successful.'	With REBT, the core belief will be disputed by changing it to: 'It would be nice to be successful but it is not absolutely necessary. I am not any less of a person if I don't succeed.'	With CBT: 'I am not worthless, just because I failed an exam.' With REBT: 'I am not worthless, just because I am not successful.'

CBT will challenge (dispute) inferences, with the aim of changing them by a process of 'disputation'. For REBT, the disputation is toward the core beliefs and the objective of this type of therapy is to change core beliefs. Both therapies are trying to achieve an 'effective new belief', so the symptoms of the client can be relieved, via a process of improved belief about the activating event and therefore adaptive behaviour that alleviates stress.

CBT: Stress inoculation therapy

Stress Inoculation Therapy (SIT) developed by Meichenbaum (1996) enables the client to be inoculated, or shielded, from the things that cause them stress, both in the present and the future. The shield is created by giving the client alternative views of experiences and arming them with coping skills, so they are more able to tackle challenging situations as they arise.

The therapy comprises three main stages:

Conceptualisation
This is a collaborative process. The therapist gets to know the person using a variety of methods, such as interviewing, as well as observing their thought processes and behaviour. The therapist will begin to challenge those thought processes, helping the client use existing knowledge effectively, and encouraging new ways of thinking about a situation. Clients are encouraged to view perceived threats as problems-to-be-solved and to identify the difference between what can and cannot be changed. Clients are shown how to break big stressors down into smaller achievable goals, over various time periods. In essence, the therapist is beginning to reconceptualise the client's stress responses.

Skills acquisition and practice
The therapist teaches the client new skills, practised in the safe setting of the clinic, using scenarios similar to the sort of situations the client finds challenging. New coping skills

might include cognitive restructuring (processing problems differently), self-soothing and acceptance, interpersonal skills training (learning how to deal with others differently) and relaxation training.

Application

The client has the opportunity to apply the newly-acquired skills, firstly through techniques such as imagery and role playing, and then real-life experience. The client will be helped in identifying triggers to risky situations for them, and to prepare for them in their own unique way (inoculation), so they have ownership of their coping skills. There are also 'follow through' bonus sessions to give reassurance and consolidate skills in a safe environment, in order to prevent relapse.

Evaluation

Strengths

➤ Both CBT and REBT are tailored to the individual.

➤ They are very effective in treating depression and moderately effective in treating anxiety disorders, particularly panic disorders

➤ There are no significant side effects, as in drug therapy.

Weaknesses

➤ Ethically, the therapy does imply the client's disorder or problem is their own fault, which may increase stress.

➤ It is also possible that, due to individual circumstances, it is rational to have negative belief systems e.g. it has been suggested that perhaps depressed people have a realistic view of the world, rather than a negative irrational view

Research

The effectiveness of CBT has been demonstrated on adult and juvenile offenders in reducing recidivism (re-offending, that is breaking the law again). This has been shown with research evidence such as the meta-analysis covering 69 studies by Pearson et al (2002), where the studies compared recidivism rates between prisoners receiving behaviour therapy, such as token economy or were on a CBT programme. The analysis of findings showed CBT to be more effective in reducing recidivism (30% rate).

A study looking at the effectiveness of using CBT for back pain by Lamb et al (2010) found after a year CBT had shown a sustained positive effect on lower back pain.

References

BECK, A. T. (1967) *Depression: Causes and Treatment*. Philadelphia: University of Pennsylvania Press.

BEIDEL, D. C. & TURNER, S. M. (1986) A Critique of the Theoretical Bases of Cognitive Behavioural Theories and Therapy. Clinical *Psychology Review*. 6. pp.177–97.

ELLIS, A. (1962). *Reason and Emotion in Psychotherapy*. New York: Stuart.

LAMB, S. et al (2010) Group Cognitive Behavioural Treatment for Low-Back Pain in Primary Care: a randomised controlled trial and cost-effectiveness analysis, *The Lancet*, "http://www.thelancet.com/journals/lancet/issue/vol375no9718/PIIS0140-6736%2810%29X6117-7". 13 March; 375 (9718). 916–923.

LEWINSOHN, P. et al (1981) Depression Related Cognitions: Antecedent or Consequences? *Journal of Abnormal Psychology*. 90. pp.213–9.

MEICHENBAUM, D. (1996). Stress Inoculation Training for Coping with Stressors. *The Clinical Psychologist*. 49. pp.4–7.

PEARSON, F. S. et al (2002) The Effects of Behavioral/Cognitive, Behavioral Programs on Recidivism.*Crime and Delinquency*. 48 (3). pp.476–96.

Therapies: psychoanalysis

Psychoanalysis, developed by Freud, aims to provide the client with personal insight in order to ensure more self-control. Bringing unconscious unresolved conflicts into the conscious enables those repressed thoughts to be freed and resolved. Psychoanalysis includes Freud-driven techniques such as hypnosis, free association and dream analysis. It now also includes neo-Freudian techniques such as ego analysis, psychodrama, play therapy, transactional analysis and interpersonal psychotherapy.

Freud-driven techniques

Freud believed that a cure for a psychological disorder could only be achieved when the cause of the problem has been addressed, as well as the symptoms being treated. Therapies work on the basis that abnormal behaviour is due to repressed conflicts in the unconscious that threaten the ego.

The function of repression, which is an ego defence mechanism, is to reduce anxiety in the conscious mind. The repressed conflicts cause the person to regress back to the stage at which they were fixated, causing a variety of mental illnesses. The original psychoanalysis aimed to work through the repressed thoughts in the unconscious by bringing them into the conscious mind.

Free association
The therapist introduces a topic and the client is free to talk of whatever comes to mind. Fragments of repressed thoughts will hopefully emerge and the therapists will be able to help free the thoughts, so they can be dealt with. The client is often resistant to allowing their mind to wander, but the skilled therapist will be able to interpret the silences, that will give clues to the unconscious conflicts.

Dream analysis
The unconscious repressed thoughts are revealed through dreams. According to Freud, there were two parts to

dreams: manifest content (the dream that is seen) and latent content (the underlying repressed thoughts that the manifest content is representing symbolically). He called dreams 'the royal road to the unconscious'. Jung's theory of dreams (1948) was slightly different, as he felt dreams were merely reflections of unresolved problems.

In both Freud's and Jung's dream analysis, the client writes their dreams in a notebook and the therapist analyses the content to discover the workings of the unconscious mind.

Hypnosis

In his early work, Freud used hypnosis as a means of accessing the unconscious. However, he ceased to use it due to the unreliability of information extracted from the hypnotic state. Also, it is not always possible to hypnotise people.

Hypnosis has had something of a revival in recent years, but remains problematic for the same reasons.

Criticisms of Freud-driven techniques

Falsifiability

If a client agrees with their therapist's analysis, there is no problem. If the client rejects the analysis, it is because they are displaying resistance to treatment and the therapist is still correct. This means the analysis cannot be falsified, because the therapist is right, even when they are wrong.

Appropriateness

Sloan et al (1975) found that psychoanalysis only really works on clients with less severe problems (neurosis). Garfield (1992) suggested that this type of therapy was only suitable for certain types of people, finding that 'Young, Attractive, Verbally skilled, Intelligent and Successful' (YAVIS) people were those that most benefitted.

Another problem could be of money and time, as these traditional types of psychoanalysis can take months or even years and are very expensive.

Effectiveness
Eysenck (1952) analysed two studies into the effectiveness of this type of therapy and found around 66% of the control group (those who had no treatment) spontaneously improved, while around 44% of the treatment group improved with treatment. However, Bergin (1971) re-analysed the same studies, but using different outcome criteria, and found that therapy was actually around 83% successful compared to the control group's spontaneous recovery rate of around 30%.

Neo-Freudian techniques

The newer therapies, although applicable and accessible to more people, still aim to access repressed unresolved conflict.

Ego analysis
This modification of psychoanalysis developed and used by Anna Freud, Karen Horney and Erik Erikson. It concentrates on strengthening the ego (conscious rational mind), rather than on conflicts in the unconscious. It also focuses on current interpersonal and social conflicts, rather than on past childhood experiences.

Psychodrama
This therapy was developed by Moreno (1946). It allows the client to show deep emotional and irrational feelings in a safe environment by acting out their emotions, and to work through them in an objective way. In this type of therapy people also write stories and use art to express themselves.

Play therapy

Play therapy was developed for children and allows them to work through their issues of conflict and repressed emotions through play, for example using dolls to demonstrate their own feelings. Play therapy has broadened out from the psychodynamic approach and has increased in importance since the 1980s as an important therapy for children.

Transactional analysis (TA)

This adaptation from psychoanalysis is again concerned with the present, rather than childhood experience. Berne (1964) proposed three ego states: child (impulsive), adult (rational) and parent (representing social inhibition). Most normal social interaction uses adult-adult, but this line can get crossed, if one person is manipulating another. TA uses role play to help people uncross the lines, leading to a healthier way of interacting with others.

Interpersonal psychotherapy (IPT)

The theory behind IPT was part of the origin of the community mental health movement. It pulled away from the traditions of the Freudian approach and looked toward the interactions clients had with others, as the key to mental health. Much of the work involved adults with depression, and it has gone on to be used with adolescent and geriatric patients with some success. IPT combines psychodynamic theory, by looking at the underlying causes of deficits in a client's interactions with others, with cognitive-behavioural theories. It has a time limit (12–16 weeks) and uses homework tasks, structured interviews and other psychometric tests. It is in reality a multi-dimensional approach therapy, combining the best of each approach.

There are three stages to treatment:

1. Therapist and client identify problems and create a treatment contract together, so a collaborative process.

2. The identified problems are worked through, and generally fall into four categories: grief reaction, role dispute (how client Interacts with others), role transition (the client is moving from one role to another e.g. retiring/redundancy) and interpersonal deficits (looking at poor social skills and difficulties forming/maintaining relationships).

3. Consolidation of what has been learnt, and help to apply new knowledge to present and future situations.

Evaluation of neo-Freudian techniques

Interpersonal psychotherapy has been shown to produce results comparable to CBT and drug therapy in cases of depression, and produces a quicker improvement in IP functioning than other therapies (Elkin et al, 1989)

It would seem it is not time to write off psychodynamic therapies, as many have, but to see how the newer versions of therapy develop, such as TA and IPT. These therapies have been shown to be versatile and effective.

Research

Elkin et al (1989) carried out the largest study on effectiveness of treatment for depression in the USA, involving 250 participants and lasting four months. The participants were randomly assigned to one of four treatment groups: IPT, CBT, imipramine (tricyclic drug) and placebo (control group). The drug groups (imipramine and placebo) also had minimal support, as it would have been unethical not to give any support to depressed patients.

The findings showed no significant difference between the IPT, CBT and imipramine groups, with a significant improvement of symptoms, albeit over different time scales. The placebo group also showed some limited improvement. IPT was shown to be more effective than CBT on clients with more severe symptoms. On follow up 18 months later, the clients who had received IPT and CBT felt they were better equipped to form and maintain relationships, which helped them understand their depression better.

Case study: psychodrama

Annie has a problem spending too much money. She seems addicted to shopping, to the extent that her flat is overflowing with clothes, shoes and handbags. She is in danger of losing her flat, as she cannot pay her rent , having already had her home repossessed. And still she shops.

A neo-Freudian therapy that might help Annie is psychodrama, where she would be able to talk to herself from an objective view point, which would also help her to help herself to a degree. ITP might help her establish healthy communication with people she would like to be closer to, which in turn could help her understand and resolve her problems more easily.

References

BERGIN, A. E. (1971) The Evaluation of Therapeutic Outcomes. In BERGIN, A. E. & GARFIELD, S. L. (eds.) *Handbook of Psychotherapy and Behaviour Change*. pp.217–70. New York: Wiley.

ELKIN, I. et al (1989). National Institute of Mental Health Treatments of Depression Collaborative Research Program: General effectiveness of treatments. *Archives of General Psychiatry*. 46. pp.971–82.

EYSENCK, H. J. (1952) The Effects of Psychotherapy: An Evaluation. *Journal of Consulting Psychology.*, 16. pp.319–24.

FREUD, A. (1966) The Ego and the Mechanisms of Defence. Revised edition. New York: International Universities Press, Inc. (First edition published in 1936.)

GARFIELD, S. (1992) Response to Hans Eysenck. In DRYDEN, W. & FELTHAM, C. (eds.) *Psycholotherapy and its discontents*. Buckingham: Open University Press.

SLOAN, R. B. et al (1975) *Psychotherapy versus Behaviour Therapy*. Cambridge, MA: Harvard University Press.

Index

A

adrenaline 181, 182, 183, 190
agency theory 136–7
aggression 15, 16, 25, 26, 70, 84, 105, 158–9, 176–8
   'Bobo doll' study 5, 176–7
   stress and 185, 190
agoraphobia 89, 90, 94
altruism 18
animal research 4, 17, 32, 52–4, 149, 152–3
anomalistic psychology 139–42, 168, 169
anorexia nervosa 56, 195
ANS (autonomic nervous system) 90–1, 107, 181, 182–4, 184, 188
anxiety 4, 77, 84, 87, 88, 89, 90–1, 137, 206, 208
   and memory recall 104, 112, 113, 116
   see also CBT; phobias
attachment 17, 40, 45
   disruption and privation 34–9
   formation 30–3, 38, 44–5
   types 40–6
autonomic nervous system see ANS
aversion therapy 193

B

Bandura, Albert 5, 68–9, 93, 176–8, 180
Bartlett 125, 127
Beck, Aaron 203, 204
   cognitive triad 11, 81
behavioural approach 2–3, 3, 4–6, 22, 68, 69, 74, 154, 203
   to attachment 32
   to OCD 87
   to phobias 91–2, 94
behavioural therapies 193–7
biases 37, 100, 114, 158
   culture bias 44, 75, 76, 100, 100–1, 102
   gender bias 76, 100, 101–2
   investigator bias 155, 164
   participant bias 44, 155, 163–4
   social desirability 37, 164

biological approach 3, 7–9, 14, 68, 72, 74, 154
   to depression 78–80
   to phobias 90–1, 94
   to schizophrenia 98–9
biological rhythms 47–51
biological therapies 2, 198–202
bipolar disorder 76, 77–8, 78
'Bobo doll' study 5, 176–7
Bowlby, John 17, 30–1, 32–3, 34, 35–7, 45
BPS (British Psychological Society) 149–51, 153, 168
brain 10, 80, 86, 118, 141, 199–200, 201, 202
   structure 80, 99
   see also sleep
brain plasticity theory of sleep 173–4
British Psychological Society see BPS

C

case studies 11, 19, 28, 29, 154, 157
CBT (cognitive behavioural therapy) 13, 83, 88, 93, 186, 203–7, 212, 212–13
CCT (client-centred therapy) 20–1
Chomsky, Noam 10, 73
CI (cognitive interview) technique 108–11, 127
circadian rhythm 47, 49, 51
classical conditioning 4, 52–6, 60, 87, 91, 92, 193–5
client-centred therapy see CCT
clinical depression see MDD
cognitive approach 3, 10–13, 69, 74, 87–8, 154, 180, 203
   to phobias 92–3, 94
   to schizophrenia 98
cognitive behavioural therapy see CBT
cognitive interview technique see CI
conditioning 87, 91–2, 93–4, 180
   classical 4, 52–6, 60, 87, 91, 92, 193–5
   operant 5, 6, 52, 57–60, 69, 87, 91–2, 195–6
conformity 61–7

conscious mind 24, 25, 121, 208, 210
consciousness, levels of 24, 25
consistency 64, 65–6
coping 185, 186, 187, 188, 205–6
corticosteroids 182, 183–4
cortisol 79, 182, 183
crime, and heredity 70
cue dependency 119–20, 132
culture 42–3, 70, 90, 126
culture bias 44, 75, 76, 100, 100–1, 102

D

Darwin, Charles 14, 72
data types 143–5, 154, 156, 158
defence mechanisms 26, 121
depression 11, 23, 76–83, 106, 187, 199–200, 201
   drug therapies 79, 81–2, 83, 106, 172–3, 198, 201, 212–13
   psychological therapies 82, 83, 106, 206, 211–13
   serotonin and 50, 79, 106
depression inventory 204
deprivation 34, 34–5, 38
desensitisation, systematic 107, 194, 196
determinism 22, 68, 68–9, 70
   reciprocal 179, 180
development 24, 26–9, 30, 31, 35–6, 73
disruption 34, 37, 38, 39, 44
dopamine 79, 99
dreams 141, 208–9
drug therapies 3, 8, 105, 198–9
   for depression 79, 81–2, 83, 106, 172–3, 198, 201, 212–13
   for OCD 86
DSM 37, 84, 85, 90, 97, 161, 162
dual process theory 66–7

E

eating disorders 56, 195
ecological theory of sleep 170–1
ecological validity 43, 60, 66, 113, 132, 138, 155, 156, 163
ECT (electro-convulsive therapy) 82, 199–200

Index

EEA (environment of evolutionary
 adaptiveness) 16–17, 72
encoding specificity principle
 108, 120
endocrine system 7–8, 107, 181,
 182–4, 188
endogenous pacemakers see EPs
environment 4–6, 9, 15, 17–18,
 44, 94, 98, 99, 105, 190
 for experiments 164
environment of evolutionary
 adaptiveness see EEA
EPs (endogenous pacemakers)
 47, 49
ERP (exposure and response
 prevention therapy) 87
ethical issues 44, 92, 149–53, 155,
 193, 200, 206, 212
 animal research 60, 105,
 152–3
 Milgram study 138, 151
'eustress' 188
evolution
 of the mind 16–18
 theory of 14–16, 72
evolutionary approach 14–18,
 170–1
EWT (eye witness testimony)
 104–5, 108–11, 112–16,
 126–7
exhaustion 182, 184
exogenous zeitgebers see EZs
experiments 10–11, 19, 155–6,
 158–9
 laboratory 6, 7, 60, 104–5,
 112, 131, 137–8, 155,
 159, 163
exposure and response prevention
 therapy (ERP) 87
eye witness testimony see EWT
EZs (exogenous zeitgebers) 47,
 49, 50

F
fear, hierarchy of 194, 196
flashbulb memories 120–1
flooding 194–5
forgetting 117–21
fraud, scientific 168–9
free will 68, 69, 69–70, 70
Freud, Sigmund 24–9, 87, 106
 therapies 208–10
 see also psychoanalysis

G
gambling 6, 59
GAS (General Adaptation
 Syndrome) 183–4
gender 27, 90, 178
gender bias 76, 100, 101–2
genes 7, 9, 14, 18, 44, 72, 73–4
genetic explanations 7, 15, 70
 crime 70
 depression 78–9, 81
 OCD 86
 phobias 91, 94
 schizophrenia 98–9
 sleep 175
Gestalt therapy 21, 106

H
hardy personality 185, 186, 188
hierarchy of fear 194, 196
hierarchy of needs 19–20
holistic approach 75, 106
hormones 7–8, 79, 105, 107, 181,
 182–4, 198
 see also adrenaline;
 dopamine; melatonin;
 noradrenaline
humanist approach 19–23, 70,
 74, 154
hypothalamus 181, 182
hypotheses 141, 154, 157–8, 166,
 167, 168, 171
hypothetico-deductive method
 132, 155, 166, 171

I
idiographic approach 19, 22, 154
implosion 194–5
information-processing approach
 3, 10–13, 122–4, 129–33
infradian rhythm 47, 50
insomnia 172–3, 173, 175, 199
intelligence 17–18, 69, 75, 102,
 160
investigator bias 155, 164
IPT (interpersonal psychotherapy)
 29, 82, 211–13
IQ (intelligence quotient) 75,
 148, 160

J
Jung, Carl 209

L
laboratory experiments 6, 7, 60,
 104–5, 112, 131, 137–8,
 155, 159, 163
language 10, 35, 60, 73
leading questions 112, 114,
 115–16
learned helplessness 80
learning 4–6, 130, 174, 176
learning theory see behavioural
 approach
levels of consciousness 24, 25
levels of measurement 143–5
levels of processing 122–4, 133
Little Albert 4, 55, 92
Little Hans 28–9
Locke, John 73
locus of control 135–6, 136, 185,
 186–7, 188
Loftus, Elizabeth 104–5, 112,
 112–13, 115–16, 116
Lorenz, Konrad 17, 31
LTM (long-term memory) 117,
 118–20, 129, 130–2, 174
 see also reconstructive
 memory

M
major depressive disorder see MDD
majority influence 61–3, 66–7
manic depression see bipolar
 disorder
Maslow, Abraham 19–20, 68
MDD (major depressive disorder)
 76–7, 77–8, 78–80, 81, 83
MDH (maternal deprivation
 hypothesis) 35–7
melatonin 8, 47, 49, 50
memes 18
memory 10, 106, 176, 180
 eye witness testimony 104–5,
 108–11, 112–16, 126–7
 forgetting 117–21
 levels of processing 122–4,
 133
 long-term see LTM
 models of 10, 105–6, 122–4,
 129, 133
 reconstructive 108, 109, 112,
 125–8
 short-term see STM
 structure 129–33

menstrual cycle 50, 77, 145
micro-organisms explanation of
    behaviour 9, 72
Milgram, Stanley
    agency theory 136–7
    obedience study 134, 134–5,
        137–8, 151, 159
mind
    evolution of 17–18
    theory of 25
minority influence 63–5, 66–7
monotropic bond 30–2, 33, 34, 44
mundane realism 132, 155, 156

N

nature, and nurture 72–5, 180
NDEs (near-death experiences)
    139–41
needs, hierarchy of 19–20
negative self-schemas 11–12, 81
neo-Freudian techniques 210–13
neurotransmitters 7–8, 79, 105,
    107, 173, 198
nomothetic approach 19, 22, 154
non-humans 4, 17, 32, 52–4, 105,
    149, 152–3
noradrenaline 79, 81, 82, 106,
    181, 183, 190
nurture, nature and 72–5, 180

O

obedience 134–8
OBEs (out-of-body experiences)
    139, 140, 141–2
obesity 17, 56, 195
OCD (obsessive-compulsive
    disorder) 84–8, 198,
    201, 202
operant conditioning 5, 6, 52,
    57–60, 69, 87, 91–2, 195–6
out-of-body experiences see OBEs

P

participant bias 44, 155, 163–4
Pavlov's dogs 52–4
PCT (person-centred therapy) 20–1
perception 10, 23, 24, 115–
    16, 203
personality 22, 24, 32–3, 134, 136
    and stress 185–6, 187–8
    theory of 25
phobias 4, 55, 56, 60, 89–95, 196
    treatment 107, 194–5, 196

placebos 201, 212–13, 213
play therapy 29, 211
primary memory 122–3
privation 34–5, 38, 44, 72
pseudo-science 166, 166–8, 169
psychoanalysis 24, 26, 82, 87,
    208–13
psychodrama 210, 213
psychodynamic approach 2–3, 3,
    22, 24–9, 68, 74, 82, 154,
    211, 212
    to OCD 86–7
    to phobias 94
psychology
    anomalistic 139–42, 169
    approaches to 2–29, 154
psychopathology 20, 74
psychosexual stages of
    development 26–9
psychosurgery 201, 202
psychotherapy 22, 73, 105, 106,
    198, 199
    see also CBT; REBT
punishment 57, 58–9, 69, 178

Q

Q-sort method 21–2, 22
qualitative methods 154, 156–9
quantitative methods 7, 11,
    154–6, 158, 158–9
questionnaires 28, 155, 157,
    157–8, 159, 160, 165

R

RAD (reactive attachment disorder)
    37
REBT (rational-emotive behaviour
    therapy) 203, 204,
    204–5, 206
reciprocal determinism 179, 180
reconstructive memory 108, 109,
    112, 125–8
reductionism 6, 104–7, 155
reinforcement 57, 58–9, 87,
    91–2, 195
    vicarious 178, 180
reliability 66, 76, 92, 131, 160–2
repression 26, 87, 121, 208
research
    data types 143–5
    design 146–8
    methods 154–9
    see also ethical issues;
        reliability; validity

restoration theories of sleep
    171–3, 175
Rogers, Carl 19, 20–1, 68
Rosenhan, David, diagnosis study
    161–2

S

SAD (seasonal affective disorder)
    8, 50
schemas 11–12, 81, 114, 125–6,
    127
schizophrenia 9, 96–9, 105
    therapies 195, 196, 198, 199
science 12, 19, 166, 167–8
scientific fraud 168–9
SCT (Social Cognitive Theory) 179
seasonal affective disorder see SAD
self-efficacy 179, 180
semantic processing 122, 123
separation 34, 36–7
serotonin 8, 47, 86, 173, 199
    and depression 50, 79, 81,
        82, 106
short-term memory see STM
SIT (stress inoculation therapy)
    204, 205–6
Skinner, B.F. 5, 57, 59, 69, 73, 195
'Skinner box' 5, 57
sleep 8, 48, 49, 50, 51, 170–5,
    190
SLT (social learning theory) 5, 10,
    68–9, 92, 176–80
snowball effect 65
social anxiety disorder 89, 90,
    91, 92
social cognitive theory (SCT) 179
social desirability bias 37, 164
social learning theory see SLT
social phobia 89, 90, 91, 92
'Stanford prison experiment'
    151, 159
statistics 143
stereotyping 126, 164
STM (short-term memory) 10,
    117, 117–18, 118, 120–2,
    123, 129
'Strange Situation' study 40–4
stress 7, 12, 23, 79, 80, 89,
    139, 185
    bodily responses 181–4
    individual differences 12,
        185–9
    in the workplace 190–2

Index

see also exhaustion; PTSD
stress inoculation therapy *see* SIT
stress-related illness 68, 184,
    185–6, 187–8
studying 123–4
systematic desensitisation 107,
    194, 196

T
TA (transactional analysis) 29,
    211, 212
temperament hypothesis 44–5
therapies 2, 13, 74
    behavioural 193–7
    biological 2, 198–202
    client-centred 20–1
    Gestalt therapy 21, 106

psychoanalysis 82, 208–13
psychotherapy 22, 73, 106,
    107, 198, 199
    see also CBT; depression;
    drug therapies; OCD
Thorndike's puzzle box 57
transactional analysis *see* TA
transactional model of stress
    12, 185
twins 7, 9, 78, 79, 91, 168

U
ultradian rhythm 47, 48, 51
unconscious mind 3, 24, 25, 26,
    82, 121, 208, 209
unipolar depression *see* MDD

V
validity 66, 76, 131, 155, 157,
    160, 162–5
    see also ecological validity
vicarious reinforcement 178, 180

W
'War of the Ghosts' study 127
workplace stress 190–2

Y
Yerkes-Dodson Law 104, 113, 116

Z
Zimbardo, Philip et al. 151, 159

Dedication

This book is dedicated to three of the most special and important men in my life, my Dad, John Flint who died too young and my sons, Ian and Adam.